THE MORE DIVINE PROOF

American Academy of Religion
Academy Series

edited by
Susan Thistlethwaite

Number 69
THE MORE DIVINE PROOF
Prophecy and Inspiration in Celsus and Origen
by
Robert J. Hauck

Robert J. Hauck

THE MORE DIVINE PROOF
Prophecy and Inspiration
in Celsus and Origen

Scholars Press
Atlanta, Georgia

THE MORE DIVINE PROOF
Prophecy and Inspiration in Celsus and Origen

by
Robert J. Hauck

© 1989
The American Academy of Religion

Library of Congress Cataloging in Publication Data

Hauck, Robert John, 1954-
    The more divine proof / Robert J. Hauck.
    p. cm. -- (American Academy of Religion academy series ; no.
69)
    Originally presented as the author's thesis (Ph.D., Duke
University, 1985) under title: Inspiration as apologetic.
    Includes bibliographical references.
    ISBN 1-55540-415-4 (alk. paper). -- ISBN 1-55540-416-2 (pbk. :
alk. paper)
    1. Origen. Contra Celsum. 2. Celsus, Platonic philosopher, fl.
180. 3. Prophecy (Christianity)--History of doctrines--Early
church, ca. 30-600. 4. Prophecy--History. 5. Christianity and
other religions--Greek. 6. Authority (Religion)--History of
doctrines--Early church, ca. 30-600. 7. Bible--Inspiration--History
of doctrines--Early church, ca. 30-600. 8. Inspiration--Religious
aspects--History of doctrines--Early church, ca. 30-600. I. Title.
II. Series.
BR65.O56H38   1989
231.7'45--dc20   89-27533
                                                   CIP
            Printed in the United States of America
                     on acid-free paper

For my father,

Gordon R. Hauck
1923 - 1977

Table of Contents

Acknowledgments

I would like to express my gratitude to those who helped this book come to completion. Special thanks are due to Robert C. Gregg, who directed my Duke University dissertation and provided inestimable advice, support, and encouragement; and Franklin W. Young, for his ideas and insight at the inception of this project. My gratitude also goes to my colleagues at Converse College, David Schenck and Malinda Maxfield, who read the manuscript, gave sound advice, and helped me over many obstacles. Rita Weeks provided invaluable service in proofing the typescript, and my thanks for their generous help in the preparation of the manuscript go to Katrina Chandler, Janet Hauck, Kitty Mackey, and Mary Overcash. A special debt of gratitude is owed to Janet and John, without whose love, encouragement, and forbearance this book would not have been possible.

Chapter 1

Introduction

> From every point of view, therefore, it must
> be seen that in no other way than only from
> the prophets who teach us by divine
> inspiration, is it at all possible to learn
> anything concerning God and the true
> religion. *Coh. Gr. 38.*

THE QUESTION

The author of the above extract from the *Exhortation to the Greeks*
sums up his apology and presents what he considers to be his most
telling point: the issue between pagan and Christian depends upon
prophecy and inspiration.[1] It is a suitable summary, for the issue of
prophecy and inspiration was central to the apologetic literature which
preceded him.[2] He also expresses a point of agreement between pagan

---

[1] Abbreviations of ancient works follow the *Oxford Classical Dictionary*, and
the *Patristic Greek Lexicon*. For editions and translations of ancient works used
in this book, see the Bibliography.

[2] A. Hilary Armstrong, "The Self-Definition of Christianity in Relation to Later
Platonism," in *Jewish and Christian Self-Definition*, vol. 1, *The Shaping of
Christianity in the Second and Third Centuries*, ed. E.P. Sanders (Philadelphia:
Fortress, 1982), pp. 84-88.

and Christian; the question was often not whether prophecy was helpful or necessary in the quest for divine knowledge, but where true prophecy was to be found. E. R. Dodds' observation about the discussion of miracles in antiquity applies equally well to the debate over prophecy; it "was in the main not a debate between believers and rationalists, but between two sorts of believers."[3] Both pagan and Christian had a long tradition dealing with the issues of prophecy, inspiration, and the knowledge of God.

On the Christian side, the outlines of this discussion have long been clear. The Christian apologists argued that believers had been illuminated by the proclamations of the Old Testament prophets, and the proof of their prophecy was to be found in the antiquity of their teaching and the fulfillment of their predictions. However, in debate "between believers," such assertions are often built on underpinnings which are plain to the combatants but obscure to outsiders. To understand the conflict between pagan and Christian, we must examine these underpinnings. As the Christian apologists made their exclusive claim to divine truth, we must ask to what extent, and in what fashion, they engaged the pagan tradition on prophecy, and try to determine which facets of the prophet's experience were considered telling in the discussion of either side. We must ask what the disputants' concept of inspiration and prophecy was, what role this understanding played in the struggle between pagan and Christian, and upon what justification each rejected the inspiration claims of their opponent.

Perhaps the best place to begin to answer such questions is the *Against Celsus* of Origen. Here are presented the arguments of both the pagan critic and the Christian apologist; and here it is clear that both are concerned with the problem of inspiration. Celsus, the defender of an age-old "true doctrine" which has existed throughout the ages, finds the source of this doctrine in "inspired poets, philosophers and wise men" (*Cels.* 7.41). Origen must attack the valued place of oracles in Greek culture and Celsus' appeals to inspiration, and defend the Christian reliance upon the special revelation to be found in the prophets and Christ. The question of trustworthy divine knowledge is one of the

---

[3] E.R. Dodds, *Pagan and Christian in an Age of Anxiety*, (New York: W.W. Norton, 1965), p. 124.

focal points of the debate represented by *Against Celsus*, and the arguments of both sides provide a unique opportunity for examining the views of both concerning prophecy and inspiration. This study, therefore, will examine the use of concepts of inspiration as apologetic tools. We will first of all deal with the background of prophecy, inspiration, and polemic in the hellenistic world, and then consider how Celsus and Origen defend their reliance on the inspired figures of their traditions, and how they attempt to discredit the claims to divine wisdom made by the other. We will follow in the thought of Origen and Celsus such issues as the psychology of inspiration, the problem of daemonic influence,[4] and the distinction between true and false prophets.

The thesis of this study is that the question of prophetic knowledge is central to what holds pagan and Christian apart, and indeed, is an important facet of late antique religious thought. The ultimate question is how the soul finds freedom from the powers which seek to restrain it. Both Celsus and Origen argue that their own founders achieved such liberation. Both want to prove that divine truth is found in their own traditions; both assert that the teachers of the other's doctrine were misled by false and daemonic inspiration; both claim that their founders were inspired sages, who rose above earthly limits to find the knowledge of God. Both sides, pagan and Christian, are concerned with the mechanics of prophecy: how and when it occurs, what is the source of the inspiring influence; and most importantly, whether it is bound to earth by daemons, or ascended to heaven with the souls of divine men. This issue thus provides an entree to the fundamental religious questions of late antiquity.[5]

The goal of this study is therefore to provide an examination of this issue within its own context, with special attention to the factors considered important by the participants in the debate. Past approaches to the question of prophecy have often neglected the immediate context

---

[4]Throughout this study, *daemon* instead of *demon* will be used to describe intermediate spiritual beings and to include pagan understandings of the term, which, unlike the Christian doctrine associated with the term *demon*, were not consistently negative.

[5]See Peter Brown, *The Making of Late Antiquity* (Cambridge: Harvard University Press, 1978).

in favor of wider questions. Prophecy and inspiration have been widely studied from the history of religions point of view,[6] which has compared the phenomenon of inspiration over a wide range of periods and circumstances, while the history of dogma approach has often simply attempted to place the statements of early Christian figures within the broader scope of the development of the doctrine of Scripture. In addition, treatments of Celsus have often been concerned with placing him on the spectrum of rationalism/superstition, while much of the modern discussion of Origen's thought has been occupied with the question of whether Origen was an intellectual or a mystic. All of these approaches have value, but in addressing questions foreign to the second and third centuries, they may overlook the religious and intellectual ideals of their subjects, and often introduce unnecessary inconsistencies into the thought of ancient figures. This study will attempt to focus on the question as it is enunciated by Celsus and Origen, with attention to their place in the hellenistic world of the second and third centuries. It is only by dealing with the debate in its own context of apologetic, and by attempting to appreciate the issues at stake for both sides, that the concepts and contributions of Origen and Celsus to the history of inspiration may be understood.[7]

---

[6] Eric Fascher, *PROPHETES. Eine sprach- und religionsgeschichtliche Untersuchung* (Gießen: A. Töpelmann, 1927), provides the best example of this approach. More recently, David Aune has provided an exhaustive study in order to determine prophetic types and their relationship to New Testament studies, in *Prophecy in Early Christianity and the Ancient Mediterranean World,* (Grand Rapids, Mich.: William B. Eerdmans, 1983).

[7] Howard Clark Kee developed an extensive critique of the *religionsgeschichtliche* school, based upon sociology of knowledge theory, and argued that it is the "life-world" of the ancient world that must be reconstructed. The present study is sympathetic with his desire to understand the ancient world on its own terms, but does not use sociology of knowledge or linguistic theory to do so. Howard Clark Kee, *Miracle in the Early Christian World* (New Haven: Yale University Press, 1983).

PROBLEMS AND METHOD

There are certain problems inherent in undertaking this type of study. Chief among them is that of language and definition. The Greek world possessed a wide and varied history and literature dealing with prophecy, from the philosophic discussions of inspiration and the knowledge of God, to popular tales of dreams and divine men. Technical divination, prediction by means of magic, dreams, daytime visions, oracular utterances, prophetic proclamations, and the intuitive knowledge possessed by the sage all fall into different categories within the discussion of inspiration. Modern anthropologists and sociologists are at work on a taxonomy for these experiences,[8] but the ancient world possessed one as well. Cicero, in his dialogue on divination, distinguishes two kinds of prophetic experience: artificial divination, which uses omens or objects to gain knowledge of the future, and natural divination, wherein the soul gains prophetic knowledge without external aid (*Div.* 1.6.12). It is clear that in the treatments of Celsus and Origen, the central issue is the knowledge of God and divine truth, and both authors deal with a wide scope of prophetic experience insofar as it aids or inhibits the attainment of this truth. It is Cicero's latter type, in all its manifestations, that concerns Celsus and Origen in their discussion of the knowledge of God. In concordance with that discussion, this study will focus on aspects of natural prophecy, including dreams, visions, prophetic speech, and the divine knowledge to be found in the soul of the sage.

A problem facing all studies of intellectual or social history in the late antique period is that of drawing lines of influence. Although past scholarship has succeeded in defining the development of Platonism from its beginnings to Neoplatonism, the relative paucity of sources makes the identification of specific influences very difficult. Modern scholarship has tended to show that there existed a fund of thought and

---

[8]See, for example, I.M. Lewis, *Ecstatic Religion: An Anthropological Study of Spirit Possession and Shamanism* (New York: Penguin, 1971); and Robert W. Wilson, *Prophecy and Society in Ancient Israel* (Philadelphia: Fortress, 1980).

cultural experience which those who lived in the second and third
centuries, pagan, Jew, or Christian, shared in common. Scholars such
as Johannes Geffcken have indicated the difficulty of separating the
threads of argument in the apologetic of this period, and have shown
that one must often be content to attribute the themes of discussion to
the zeitgeist of the culture.[9] This is true in the discussion of prophecy,
for in the examination of Origen and Celsus it becomes clear that there
are certain issues and values common to the age. The purpose of this
study is to define those values with regard to prophecy, rather than to
unravel the threads of their origin. Lines of influence will therefore be
indicated only in a general way.

A more significant problem greets those examining the thought of
Celsus in *Against Celsus*. Celsus' *True Doctrine* is extant only in the
rebuttal of Origen, and Origen himself is not consistent in his treatment
of it. He tells us that he began by organizing the *Against Celsus*
around the main themes of the *True Doctrine*, but then altered his reply
to take up a point-by-point refutation of Celsus. The latter method was
the most fruitful in preserving the work of Celsus, but the modern
attempt to reconstruct its form and content has been viewed with
varying levels of optimism.   Various collections of the fragments of
Celsus were assembled in the 19th century, and Theodor Keim produced
a German version of the *True Doctrine* in 1873.[10] Glöckner produced a
reconstruction of the Greek text,[11] but Robert Bader demonstrated the
difficulty of reproducing a continuous text from the fragments preserved
by Origen.[12] Bader showed that Origen does not quote Celsus exactly,
but rather omits, abbreviates, and paraphrases as he responds to the
arguments of Celsus. More recently, Andresen has questioned some of
the fragments of Bader, and proposed new Celsian fragments of his

---

[9]Johannes Geffcken, *Zwei griechische Apologeten* (Leipzig: B. G.   Teubner,
1907, reprint ed., Hildesheim: Georg Olms, 1970), p. 221.

[10]Theodor Keim, *Kelsos Wahres Wort. Älteste Streitschrift antiker
Weltanschauung gegen das Christentum* (Zurich, 1873, reprint ed., Darmstadt:
Aalen, 1969).

[11]Otto Glöckner, *Celsi ΑΛΗΘΗΣ   ΛΟΓΟΣ* (Bonn: Marcus und E. Webers
Verlag, 1924).

[12]Robert Bader, *Der Ἀληθὴς Λόγος des Kelsos*, Tübinger Beiträge zur
Altertumswissenschaft, H. 33 (Stuttgart: W. Kohlhammer, 1940).

own.[13] The fragmentary nature of the *True Doctrine*, however, does not imply that its thought, and perhaps even its structure, may not be determined.[14] Bader concluded, ". . . so formen sich die einzelnen Bruchstücke doch zu einem einigermaßen zusammenhängenden Ganzen, das uns einen Ersatz für die verlorene Streitschrift des Kelsos bieten kann,"[15] and scholars such as Andresen have succeeded in defining the focus and themes of Celsus' thought. Though fragmentary, the *True Doctrine* as preserved by Origen betrays a unity which makes it susceptible to analysis. This study will proceed on the basis of the fragments identified by Henry Chadwick's edition and translation, which rest upon the work of Bader.[16]

HISTORIOGRAPHY

In general, treatments of Celsus and Origen have not focused on the issue of prophecy. With regard to Celsus, the tendency has been to view him as a rationalistic critic of Christianity. Harnack, who set the tone for subsequent evaluations of Celsus, saw him primarily as a

---

[13]Carl Andresen, *Logos und Nomos: Die Polemik des Kelsos wider das Christentum*, Arbeiten zur Kirchengeschichte, B. 30 (Berlin: Walter de Gruyter, 1955).

[14]Glöckner, Wifstrand, Bader, and Andresen all provide suggested outlines of the *True Doctrine*. Glöckner, *Celsi ΑΛΗΘΗΣ ΛΟΓΟΣ*; Albert Wifstrand, "Die wahre Lehre des Kelsos," *Bulletin de la Société Royale des Lettres de Lund* (1941-42):391-431, *Humanistiska vetenskapssamfundet i Lund. Arsberättelse* 1941/42 (Lund, 1942); Bader, *Der Αληθὴς Λόγος des Kelsos*; Andresen, *Logos und Nomos*. More recently, R. Joseph Hoffmann has produced an English translation of the *True Doctrine*, but his text does not address the questions raised by Bader, and is achieved by inserting unidentified and unjustified interpolations. See the review by Joseph W. Trigg, *Church History* 57 (1988):353-354. R. Joseph Hoffmann, *Celsus: On the True Doctrine* (New York: Oxford Unversity Press, 1988).

[15]Bader, *Αληθὴς Λόγος*, p. 38.

[16]Origen, *Contra Celsum*, trans. Henry Chadwick (Cambridge: Cambridge University Press, 1980). No similar problems exist with the text of the *Against Celsus*. This study will use the text of Koetschau. Paul Koetschau, trans., *Origenes Werke*, Band 1 and 2 (Leipzig: J.C. Hinrichs, 1899).

political philosopher, who demonstrated the dangers of Christianity to the Roman commonwealth.[17] Louis Rougier's approach is perhaps the best example of the view of Celsus primarily as a rationalist; for him, Celsus represented the *ancien* intellectual achievements, and defended them against the unquestioning and anti-intellectual faith of the Christians.[18] The arguments of Celsus are those of a philosopher appealing to rationality, against the fideism of his opponents. According to Rougier, Celsus expresses the wide tolerance of the philosopher for the Christians, but the Christian reliance on revelation, and their adherence to the Mosaic cosmogony in the face of the rational appeals of Celsus make peace impossible. "Le *Discours vrai*," he says, "inaugure le conflit séculaire de la science et de la religion."[19]

Other scholars have taken a broader view of Celsus' thought, and noted that there are aspects of the *True Discourse* that could be credited to the religious or even fideistic side. Many of these scholars, however, have viewed the religious side of Celsus as anomalistic, and seen it as inconsistent with his philosophic views.[20] An early example of this is the work of Anna Miura-Stange, who agreed with Harnack that the primary thrust of Celsus' thought was political.[21] Miura-Stange asserts that both Celsus and Origen lack unity of thought, and that

---

[17]Harnack says, "Celsus is an agnostic above all things." Adolf Harnack, *The Mission and Expansion of Christianity in the First Three Centuries*, trans. James Moffat, 2nd ed., Theological Translation Library, v. 19 and 20 (London: Williams & Norgate, 1908), v. 1, pp. 502-504.

[18]Louis Rougier, *Celse contre les Chrétiens: la réaction païenne sous l'empire Romain* (Paris: Copernic, 1977, first published, 1926).

[19]Ibid., p. 46.

[20]The view of Celsus as a rationalist often coincides with the identification of Celsus as the Epicurean friend of Lucian of Samosata, rather than as an otherwise unknown Platonist. Rougier holds this position: *Celse contre les Chrétiens*, p. 20. For a recent exponent of this view see Jacques Schwartz "Du Testament de Lévi au Discours véritable de Celse," *Revue d'histoire et de philosophe religieuses* 40 (1960):126-145. Because of the decidedly Platonic character of Celsus' thought, most modern scholars hold to the latter view; so Chadwick, *Contra Celsum*, p. xxv.

[21]Anna Miura-Stange, *Celsus und Origenes: Das Gemeinsame ihrer Weltanschauung, nach den acht Büchern des Origenes gegen Celsus*, (Gießen: Alfred Töpelmann, 1926), p. 2.

Celsus is not afraid of holding to strongly contradictory positions. One of his chief contradictions lies in his religious views. Celsus wants to depend on reason as the arbiter in the debate, but calls upon the piety and authority of the ancients. According to Miura-Stange, Celsus recognizes this as a weakness, but attacks the religion of the Christians from political considerations, not from his own religious concerns.[22] In like fashion, Pierre de Labriolle sees the thought of Celsus, who portrays himself as a philosopher, as riddled with contradictions. While he plays the skeptic in relation to religious claims, he himself holds to astrology and popular religious superstition. Labriolle says,

> Pour un polémiste qui se targue plus d'une fois d'obéir à la seule raison et qui accuse ses adversaires de se dérober à un guide si sûr, il faut avouer que Celse a de complaisances ou des fléchissements dont son rationalisme même aurait dû le mieux protéger.[23]

The complaint is that while Celsus' basic attack is rationalistic, his thought includes a belief in wonders and popular religious manifestations inconsistent with his rationalism.

Others have attempted to take a more unified view of Celsus' thought, and have sought to find a system or theme which would characterize the *True Doctrine*. Even these attempts, however, have often regarded Celsus' statements about contemporary religious practices as inconsistent with his intellectual position. Perhaps the most significant twentieth-century effort to tie together Celsus' thought is that of Wifstrand, who argued that Greek history and tradition is at the center of Celsus' attack on the Christians. Wifstrand connects the title of Celsus' work with Plato and later Platonists, and states that Celsus does not have in mind a single doctrine, but means by *true logos* that intellectual and cultural tradition which made up the common treasury of hellenism. This includes a *koinos nomos*, and is an "allgemeine Sitte und Meinung,"[24] "die harmonisierte heidnische Überlieferung von

---

[22]Ibid., p. 16.

[23]Pierre de Labriolle, *La réaction païenne: Etude sur la polémique antichrétienne du Ier au VIe siècle*, 8th ed. (Paris: L'Artisan du livre, 1942), p. 134.

[24]Wifstrand, "Die wahre Lehre," p. 398.

Gott und den Göttern."[25] This forms the *Grundanschauung* of Celsus' work, and is the basis for his rejection of Christianity. According to Wifstrand, "der Fehler der Christen besteht darin, dass sie sich absondern und sich gegen die von alters her üblichen Vorstellungen empören."[26]

Dörrie follows Wifstrand on the significance of the pagan tradition.[27] He argues, however, that the key to the conflict between pagan and Christian lies in Celsus' reliance upon school Platonism, and his consequently hostile views on revelation. According to Dörrie, Celsus absolutely denies the possibility of revelation, and argues that there is a universal and static fund of truth, to which nothing can be added by revelation. This truth is discovered by reason, operating through philosophy. Celsus, says Dörrie, affirms traditional Platonic ways of arriving at truth, which are based on the turning of the eyes of the soul away from the material and lifting them to the divine. He denies the possibility of any sort of direct divine knowledge, and criticizes the Christians for their stand on revelation. Celsus' system is thus rationalistic, with no room for wonders or prophecy, and his polemic against the Christians is founded on the authority of Platonism.

Carl Andresen, however, notes the significance of wonders and prophecy for Celsus, and attempts to find their place in the system of Celsus. His *Logos und Nomos* builds upon the work of Wifstrand. Like Wifstrand, Andresen feels that the key to Celsus' thought is his reliance upon the authority of the Greek past. Andresen goes farther than Wifstrand, however, in making history the ultimate authority in culture and philosophy. He sees an inner contradiction in the thought of Celsus, and asserts that it is resolved by the concept of history. For Andresen, Celsus' thought possesses two poles which can be characterized by the polarity between the rational and the religious, between public and private piety, and between philosophy and superstition. Celsus picks up this double stream of religious thought from Greek tradition, with one stream focusing on philosophical ways

---

[25]Ibid., p. 399.

[26]Ibid., p. 398.

[27]Heinrich Dörrie, "Die platonische Theologie des Kelsos in ihrer Auseinandersetzung mit der christliche Theologie: auf Grund von Origenes c. Celsum 7.42 ff.," *Nachrichten der Akademie der Wissenschaffen in Göttingen*, I. Philologische-historische Klasse, (1967):23-55.

of understanding God, and the other consisting of the stories of wonders, the mysteries, the animal cults of the barbarians, and reliance on the mediation of daemons. This dual stream is held together by the concept of history. According to Andresen, Celsus finds his authority in the past, and builds a historical, rather than philosophical, argument against the Christians. That which is part of the ancient tradition makes up the 'true logos,' and the Christians have gone wrong insofar as they have departed from it. Both the religious and philosophical stream make up the ancient logos, and thus the myths, miracle stories, and wonders are accepted because they have historical authority. There does exist an inner contradiction in the thought of Celsus, but he holds both poles together because they are part of the ancient logos. Andresen says,

> So sahen wir, wie die philosophische Skepsis des Kelsos gegenüber dem Wunder dadurch zurückgestellt wird, daß Kelsos sich der geschichtlichen Überlieferung beugt . . . . Die Welt der Frömmigkeit ist darin für ihn zu einer Einheit geworden, daß ihre beiden Pole (rationale Gotteserkenntnis und kultische Dämonenverehrung) von dem gleichen Strom einer altehrwürdigen Tradition leben.[28]

More recently, scholars have attempted to deal with this apparent contradiction in the thought of Celsus by using the methodology of the social sciences.[29]   Harold Remus has indicated the power of social

---

[28]*Logos und Nomos,* p. 77.

[29]Some scholars have attributed the apparent discontinuity in Celsus' thought to hellenistic culture as a whole. David Tiede has argued that the traditions in hellenistic culture concerning the figure of the divine man, which were used in propaganda concerning Moses and Jesus, were two-fold and contradictory. There existed both the ancient model of the divine man as wonder worker, whose divinity was authenticated by his extraordinary powers, and the model of divine man as sage, the philosophical ideal often projected onto the founders of the philosophical schools. According to Tiede, these two originally contradictory models were conflated in varying degrees by the time of Celsus, and thus apparent contradictions may exist in apologetic texts. Morton Smith, however, rejects Tiede's thesis, and argues that wonder claims were not appeals to a discrete divine man model, but simply directed to popular superstition, and when philosophers used them, in contradiction to their own philosophical positions, they were

groups in polemical contexts, and has shown the significance of the 'sociology of knowledge' in his analysis of *Against Celsus*.[30] Remus argues that groups tend to identify their own traditions as true, and all others as false, while in fact they may be affirming and condemning the same intellectual position. Thus Celsus can condemn wonders and prophecy as exercised among the Christians, while at the same time affirming their truth and validity when found in his own tradition. This is indeed true in polemic in the second century, for it is clear that many of the salvos fired in debate deal with the foreignness and novelty of the opponent's position. However, this methodology produces the same results as the work of Andresen, namely, that there are contradictions in the thought of Celsus on wonders and prophecy, without attempting to determine if indeed Celsus sees them as contradictions. The weakness of past treatments of Celsus has been to assume a distinction between philosophy, or in modern terms, rationality, and common Greek religious expressions, or superstition. It is not at all clear that Celsus or his contemporaries saw this distinction, and thus felt any contradiction in dealing with wonders and prophecy in the pagan tradition or that of the Christians. It is necessary to examine the thought of Celsus to determine what distinctions are important in his culture, and then see how he applies those distinctions to the issues facing him. In its examination of Celsus, this study will therefore lay aside, as much as possible, the dichotomy of rationality/superstition, and attempt to determine the categories in which Celsus himself deals with prophecy and inspiration.

The same type of debate has gone on in regard to Origen. Much of the modern discussion of Origen's thought has been taken up with whether Origen is to be viewed primarily as an intellectual, who

---

simply appealing for popular support. Both the positions of Tiede and Smith attribute a wide contradiction to antique thought. David Tiede, *The Charismatic Figure as Miracle Worker*, Society of Biblical Literature Dissertation Series, no. 1 (Missoula: Society of Biblical Literature, 1972); Morton Smith, "On the History of the Divine Man," in *Paganisme, Judaisme, Christianisme: Influences et affrontements dans le monde antique: Mélanges offerts à Marcel Simon* (Paris: Editions E. de Boccard, 1978):335-345.

[30]Harold Remus, *Pagan-Christian Conflict over Miracle in the Second Century*, Philadelphia Patristic Monograph Series no. 10. (Cambridge: Philadelphia Patristic Foundation, 1983).

produces a philosophical system, or as a mystic, who is concerned predominantly with the soul's ascension to the divine. Early in this century Eugene de Faye portrayed Origen as a philosopher with an abstract and speculative cosmology, and fundamentally intellectual concerns. According to de Faye, Origen's method, in exegesis as well as philosophical endeavor, is that of dialectic. De Faye characterized Origen's system in this way: "This conception is fundamentally speculative and metaphysical, the product exclusively of a powerful imagination guided by a bold and intrepid dialectic."[31] Origen's spiritual concerns are simply a part of an inherited Christian tradition, and all facets of his thought contribute to ". . . a state of mind that was purely intellectualistic and idealistic."[32]

Walther Völker, however, took the opposite position on Origen's spirituality. In direct contradiction of de Faye, Völker argued that Origen was a mystic at heart, concerned primarily not with an intellectual system, but with the spiritual struggle of the soul against the *pathē* and the daemons. According to Völker, the center of Origen's thought lies in the training and discipline of the soul, a long *askēsis* in which the soul is purged of its passions. At the end of this long journey the soul achieves union with God. Völker argues that Origen believes in the possibility of complete mystical union with the divine, and positively affirms the ecstatic *unio mystica*.[33] This is Origen's 'perfection-ideal,' the long inner ascension of the soul to union with God. Völker says of Origen's view of gnosis:

Bei der Gnosis handelt es sich also nicht um eine auf rationalem Wege gewonnene Erkenntnis, nicht um eine menschliche Spekulation, sondern um eine Erkenntnis, die zum Menschen kommt, die ihn erleuchtet, ihn über sich selbst hinaushebt und ihn in einen Zustand innerer Erhobenheit versetzt. Sie ist im letzten und höchtsten Sinn daher nur möglich, wenn der Mensch

---

[31] Eugene de Faye, *Origen and His Work*, trans. Fred Rothwell (New York: Columbia University Press, 1929), p. 42. See also Eugene de Faye, *Origène, sa vie, son oeuvre, sa pensée* (Paris: Editions E. Leroux, 1923-38).

[32] De Faye, *Origen*, p. 29.

[33] Walther Völker, *Das Vollkommenheitsideal des Origenes*, Beiträge zur historischen Theologie 7 (Tübingen: J.C.B. Mohr, 1931), p. 139.

ganz von Gott erfüllt ist, wenn er bereits die völlige *koinonia* oder *henosis* erreicht hat.[34]

The subsequent debate over the thought of Origen has been carried out along the lines established by de Faye and Völker, and the position of each has had its proponents. Hal Koch took up the position of de Faye in affirming that Origen's thought is motivated primarily by his philosophical system. According to Koch, de Faye is right in stating that Origen read the central themes of his thought into, rather than out of, Scripture, as well as in asserting that Origen's spiritual concerns are derived from his Christian traditions and do not harmonize with his philosophical system.[35] Koch argues that the motivating factor of Origen's thought is the issue of God's relationship to the world, and the providential education of souls. This education of souls is accomplished by God's providential care and by participation in the Logos, but in it Koch sees no spiritual warfare, no place for daemons, the devil, or mysticism, and no integral role for the doctrine of redemption. Origen's thought is a unified system organized around the concept of providence.[36]

On the other hand, Henri Crouzel, while modifying the extremes of Völker's position, has supported the view of Origen as a mystic. He says,

Son [Origen's] but est-il seulement de composer un système de pensées bien agencées, découlant les unes des autres comme des conséquences de leurs principes? Ou bien conçoit-il, par delà tout intermédiaire, concept ou raisonnement, image ou espèce intelligible, un contact direct avec l'intelligence divine suivant un mode supérieur à la condition habituelle des hommes? Nous avon delà des éléments de réponse: la nature spirituelle du

---

[34]Ibid., p. 90.

[35]Hal Koch, *Pronoia und Paideusis, Studien über Origenes und sein Verhaltnis zum Platonismus,* Arbeiten zur Kirchengeschichte 22 (Berlin: De Gruyter, 1932), p. 75-78.

[36]Koch, however, protests that he does not see Origen as an intellectualist, but primarily as a Christian and a churchman. Koch, *Pronoia und Paideusis,* p. 312.

mystère, la nécessité de la grâce et de la lumière pour connaître, l'aliment surnaturel qui change l'âme en sa propre substance.[37]

According to Crouzel, the object of the soul's knowledge is divine mystery, a mystery which escapes the normal capacities of the soul. The understanding of this mystery only comes by grace and an interior revelation, which occurs because of the soul's participation in the Logos and union with God. Against Völker, Crouzel denies that this is ecstasy, but names it rather "enstasy." Reason is not destroyed in this experience, but enlightened, as it joins with the divine. Says Crouzel, "Il n'y a pas sortie de l'intelligence, mais elle saisit Dieu dans son essence à elle."[38] Origen thus is not primarily a philosopher, but a Christian mystic, drawing his spiritual doctrines from Scripture, and seeking to bring the soul nearer to God. Crouzel states, "Le projet fondamental qui l'anime est plus celui d'un spirituel que du philosophe rationaliste qu'on a voulu découvrir."[39]

As in the case of Celsus, the persistence of this debate indicates that the distinctions under discussion are not self-evident in the thought of the third-century author. De Faye himself notes the modern difficulty in understanding the issues of the third century, and indicates that foreign distinctions are being imposed on antique culture. "Here we may remark," he says, ". . . that the questions raised by Origen are bound to fill modern minds with amazement. Not for a moment can we imagine the possibility of anyone asking them."[40] It is equally likely that Origen would be amazed at the modern questions asked of him. Crouzel has noted that the categories of intellectualism and mysticism in which the thought of Origen has been discussed are not integral to the thought of the third century. "Cette opposition si tranchée," he says, "est artificielle."[41] It is clear that Origen's thought must be examined on its own terms, as it deals with those questions which

---

[37]Henri Crouzel, *Origène et la "connaissance mystique"* (Paris: de Brouwer, 1961), p. 373.

[38]Ibid., p. 205.

[39]Ibid., p. 209.

[40]De Faye, *Origen*, p. 40.

[41]Crouzel, *La "connaissance mystique,"* p. 532.

modern minds find so unlikely. Only by laying aside our amazement is it possible to determine the issues and values important to antique culture, and to begin to understand the motivating factors in the thought of pagan and Christian. To that end, this study will examine the issues in the conflict between pagan and Christian in regard to prophecy, and attempt to understand the values significant to a culture different from our own.[42]

---

[42]Eugene V. Gallagher has approached the *Against Celsus* in this way, with regard to the question of the divine man. He rebukes the *religionsgeschichtliche* scholarship for importing issues of genre and type, and uses an anthropological framework to discover categories native to the second century. Eugene V. Gallagher, *Divine Man or Magician?: Celsus and Origen on Jesus*, Society of Biblical Literature Dissertation Series 64 (Chico, Ca.: Scholars Press, 1982).

Chapter 2

"Men of Ancient Times:"

The Hellenistic Context

> These doctrines I have set forth for men of
> intelligence. If you understand any of them
> you are doing well. And if you think that
> some spirit came down from God to foretell
> the divine truths, this may be the spirit
> which declares these doctrines. Indeed it was
> because men of ancient times were touched by
> this spirit that they proclaimed many
> excellent doctrines. *Cels. 7.45.*

Surprisingly enough, this quotation is from the pagan Celsus rather
than the Christian Origen, and it makes clear that this is indeed a debate
'between believers.' There was a wide-ranging discussion of prophecy
and inspiration in hellenistic times. Robin Lane Fox, noting that in
the second century there were philosophers serving as prophets at the
oracle sites, remarks, "In the early Christian era, 'paganism' had thus
become more than the sum of the acts performed in its cults: it had
acquired its own body of divine wisdom."[1] As several recent studies

---

[1] His thesis, *contra* Dodds, is that this interest in the divine is not so much a
late innovation due to "anxiety," as to a continuation of ancient tradition of
intercourse with the gods. Robin Lane Fox, *Pagans and Christians* (New York:
Alfred A. Knopf, 1987), p. 198.

have shown, the Christians were not the first group called upon to build a defense of miracle, wonders, and superior knowledge of God.[2] Philosophical literature, such as Plutarch's efforts to defend the Delphic oracle, and Middle-Platonic discussions of the knowledge of God deal with the theoretical aspects of inspiration, while a broad background of polemical and apologetic literature defends (or attacks) the inspiration and divine knowledge of particular divine men. Along with Plato, the inspired "man of ancient times" of the above quotation, Cicero, Plutarch, and Philo will serve as examples of the philosophical discussion. The apologetic literature will be represented by Lucian's skeptical satire of the *pseudomantis* Alexander, Philo's treatment of Moses, and Philostratus' hagiography of Apollonius of Tyana.

PHILOSOPHICAL DISCUSSIONS

Plato. Plato is not, of course, a hellenistic author. He is, however, one of those ἄνδρες παλαιοί whose heritage is claimed by both Celsus and Origen. Natural inspiration, by definition, is concerned with the knowledge of the divine, the character and abilities of the soul, and the obstacles which prevent the soul from achieving such knowledge. In all of these areas, especially during the second and third centuries, Plato is the *magister*, at least as he is read through the lenses of Middle Platonism. While Plato's treatment of divination and inspiration is neither extensive nor systematic, it touches many of the issues which occupy Celsus and Origen, namely, the character and trustworthiness of divination and dreams, the nature of inspiration, and the soul and its rise to true knowledge of reality. The most relevant texts are passages from the *Timaeus*, the *Republic*, and the *Phaedrus*.[3]

---

[2] For example, Gallagher, *Divine Man or Magician?;* and Remus, *Pagan-Christian Conflict.*

[3] This is not exhaustive. For a more comprehensive treatment see Friedrich Pfeffer, *Studien zur Mantik in der Philosophie der Antike*, Beiträge zur klassichen Philologie, H. 64 (Meisenheim am Glan: Anton Hain, 1976); and Paul Vicaire, "Platon et la divination," *Revue des études Grecques* 83 (1970):330-350.

Plato's treatment of divination varies among the dialogues, depending upon the purpose and setting of the discussion.[4] In the *Timaeus* it is treated in the cosmological myth, and is described in connection with the creation of the soul and its installation in the body (*Ti.* 69 C-72 C). The gods frame the body around the soul; the immortal, or rational, soul is in the head, separated by the neck from the lower soul, which resides in the chest. As in the *Republic*, the lower soul can be divided into parts, the "better" and "worse," separated in the abdomen by the diaphragm. The appetitive ("worse") part, whose job it is to feed the body, is situated lowest, at the navel, and farthest from the rational soul, to avoid disturbing it with its own "turmoil and din." This turmoil comes from the confusion and passion of this part; without the governing function of the rational soul, it "would be bewitched for the most part day and night by images and phantasms (εἰδώλων καὶ φαντασμάτων)."[5]

The confusion which the lower part of the soul causes is evident in the *Timaeus'* treatment of dreams. The inner fire, the source of normal vision, can also produce dream images. This fire is quelled when the eyes are closed, and dreamless sleep results when the fire is entirely quiet. Dreams, however, are the consequence of motion and images left behind when the eyes are closed. These images have no substance of their own, but are merely copies (φάντασμα) of something else (*Ti.* 52 C). Such images are formed in the lower body, produced by the appetites, and can deceive the lower part of the soul.[6] The liver is planted near the lower soul so that, moved by the intellect, it can calm the lower soul which is plagued by phantasms. Divination, however, is itself is seated in this area, "to rectify this vile part of us" (*Ti.* 71 E). Since the appetitive soul is irrational, and cannot know truth in any other way, divination is a gift from the gods to provide it with some knowledge of the truth. According to the *Timaeus*, then, divination is not a product of *nous*, but consists of images and voices perceived in

---

[4]Pfeffer says, "Platon bemüht sich nicht, die Äußerungen zu harmonisieren; sie stehen ganz im Dienste des jeweiligen Gedankenzusammenhangs." *Studien zur Mantik*, p. 18.

[5]*Ti.* 71 B.

[6]*Ti.* 70 E. See C.A. Behr, *Aelius Aristides and the Sacred Tales* (Amsterdam: Hakkert, 1968), p. 173.

the lower soul. These are judged by the mind when awake.[7] Dreams, even mantic dreams, because of their association with the lower soul and the passions of the body, are subject to confusion and deception by the images and phantoms produced by the association of the irrational soul and the body. For the *Timaeus,* therefore, divination is irrational. Socrates says, "No man achieves true and inspired divination when in his rational mind, but only when the power of his intelligence is fettered in sleep or when it is distraught by disease or by reason of some divine inspiration" (*Ti.* 70 E).

The *Republic*, in its rather short aside on the character of dreams, is somewhat more positive on the possibility of true and inspired dreams. The relevant passage in book 9 is concerned with the genesis of the tyrant, the man ruled by desires, and takes up the question of the power and origin of desire. Socrates begins by showing that the various desires within the soul may be seen in dreams, because they are unleashed by sleep. During sleep, the rational part of the soul slumbers, while the appetitive soul, freed from rational restraints, goes wild. Dreams are thus the stories of unrestrained desire, which, while the intelligence sleeps, can practice incest, bestiality, "or any foul deed of blood" (*Resp.* 571 D). For the foolish person, then, dreams, far from being a source of divine truth, are the playground for desire, and the best example of the perverting and confusing influence of the lower parts of the soul on the higher.

This influence, however, can be, and indeed ought to be, restrained. The wise person can prepare for sleep by "arousing the rational part," taming the passionate part, and lulling the appetitive part (*Resp.* 572). This frees the rational soul, allowing it, "in isolated purity to examine (αὐτὸ καθ' αὐτὸ μόνον καθαρὸν σκοπεῖν) and reach out towards and apprehend some of the things unknown to it, past, present, and future" (*Resp.* 572 A). This is not unlike the description of true philosophy in the *Phaedo*, where the soul, there unitary, separates itself from the weight and drag of the body and reaches out to reality. Socrates says there,

---

[7]Here the distinction is also made between diviners, who receive the images and voices, and prophets, who evaluate and interpret them rationally.

> When the soul makes use of the body for an inquiry, either
> through seeing or hearing or any of the other senses . . . then
> it is dragged by the body to things which never remain the
> same, and it wanders about and is confused and dizzy like a
> drunken man because it lays hold on such things. . . . But when
> the soul inquires alone by itself (αὐτὴ καθ' αὑτὴν σκοπῇ), it
> departs into the realm of the pure, the everlasting, the immortal
> and the changeless, and being akin to these it dwells always
> with them whenever it is by itself and is not hindered.[8]

In the *Republic* the rational soul achieves this solitude in sleep, when
the dreamer has "quieted the two elements in his soul and quickened the
third" (*Resp.* 572 B). Here, unlike the *Timaeus*, the inspired dream is
rational, achieved by freeing the rational soul from lower influences.
The result is that in the case where the sleeper has properly prepared for
an inspired dream, the mind is free to know not only oracular truth, that
is, the future, but truth itself (past, present and future). In such a case,
Socrates says, the sleeper, "is most likely to apprehend truth, and the
visions of his dreams are least likely to be lawless" (*Resp.* 572 B).

The *Phaedrus* puts inspiration in an even more elevated light. There,
as Socrates argues that the lover is the true philosopher, he does so in
the context of divine madness and inspiration. True love, in this
dialogue, exceeds wisdom, because the lover is mad with the gift of
madness from the gods. Divination (μαντικὴ), Socrates says, is
really prophetic madness (μανικὴ). This madness, or inspiration,
inspires the Delphic and other oracles, and is sent by the Muses to
inspire poets, but its highest form is the madness of love, which, says
Socrates,

> causes him to be regarded as mad, who, when he sees the beauty
> on earth, remembering the true beauty, feels his wings growing
> and longs to stretch them for an upward flight, but cannot do

---

[8]*Phd.* 79 C.

so, and, like a bird, gazes upward and neglects the things below.[9]

Here prophecy and inspiration are tied to the issue of the soul's knowledge. In the *Phaedrus* myth, the soul possesses wings on which it flies up to the divine regions. The wing, says Plato, partakes of the divine, that is, of the eternal verities of beauty, wisdom, and goodness (τὸ δὲ θεῖον καλόν, σοφόν, ἀγαθόν, *Phdr.* 246 E). The souls of the gods, perfectly ordered as they are, soar in heaven, enjoying blessed sights, and advancing even to the vault of heaven (*Phdr.* 247 B). Other souls, however, are dragged down to earth, where, having lost their wings, vaguely and with difficulty perceive the realities. However, that highest part of the soul, which once soared in heaven, can be reminded of those blessed sights and, through recollection (ἀνάμνησις), the wing of the soul can grow once more. This is what happens when the lover, seeing beauty on earth, and "remembering true beauty, feels his wings growing and longs to stretch them for an upward flight" (*Phdr.* 249 D). This one "separates himself from human interests and turns his attention towards the divine, [and] is rebuked by the vulgar, who consider him mad and do not know that he is inspired" (*Phdr.* 249 D). Here inspiration is the yearning of the highest part of the soul for the highest truth, and is necessary for the soul's knowledge of truth.

Plato's treatment of inspiration and the knowledge of God thus lays a groundwork for Middle-Platonic discussion in several areas. On one level, inspiration is the production of images or voices in the irrational soul which provides oracular knowledge. However, the highest inspiration involves the lifting of the soul to the intelligible realm and the vision of divine truth. The truly inspired is the wise person, whose soul, seeing beauty on earth, yearns for the Beauty above. The body and its passions are the primary obstacles to this ascension of the soul. They drag the soul down with love of the material, and produce bewitching images and phantasms in the lower soul. This provides a background for a discussion, not simply of oracular divination, but of inspiration as the rise of the soul, and the dangers inherent in this rise.

---

[9]*Phdr.* 249 D.

Cicero. Stoicism provides the other major ingredient in the hellenistic conception of prophecy and divination. If Platonism provided a world view which supported inspiration, Stoic theory, founded on the harmony of the cosmos, laid the foundation for the discussion of the details of prophetic inspiration.[10] Cicero provides a representative view of the Stoic approach to prophecy. *On Divination* presents a dialogue between Cicero's brother, Quintus, and Cicero himself, over the existence and validity of divination of all sorts. Quintus' discourse, occupying all of book 1, takes the affirmative position, and, citing such figures as Chrysippus, Cratippus, and Posidonius, gives the Stoic justification of divination.[11] Cicero responds in book 2, representing the New Academy, and the skeptical arguments of Carneades.[12]

As we have indicated, Quintus divides divination into two categories, artificial and natural. Although the focus of our examination is natural divination, both types of divination occur by the association of the seer's soul with the divine. Quintus' arguments center on the natural divinatory powers of the soul and its divine origin, inspiration as the motion or stirring of the soul, and the necessity of preparation of the soul for inspiration.

Natural divination can be called natural, according to Quintus, because the soul naturally possesses the power of divination. "Therefore the human soul," he says, "has an inherent power of presaging or of foreknowing infused into it from without" (*Div.* 1.31.66). This is a natural power within the soul, "inherent" in it, which provides prophetic capabilities. It is properly called a power of

---

[10]Brenk says, "Between Plato's ingenuity and Plutarch's eclecticism stands the full ponderous weight of Stoicism in unbending affirmation of the belief in divination." Frederick E. Brenk, *In Mist Apparelled: Religious Themes in Plutarch's Moralia and Lives* (Leiden: E. J. Brill, 1977), p. 209.

[11]However, Dulaey also notes the importance of Pythagoreanism in the discussion of prophecy and in eclectic Stoicism, pointing out that Quintus cites the Pythagoreans and Plato more often than he does Posidonius. Martine Dulaey, *La rêve dans la vie et la pensée de Saint Augustin* (Paris: Etudes Augustinennes, 1973), p. 23.

[12]See François Guillaumont, *Philosophe et augure. Recherches sur la théorie Cicéronienne de la divination* (Bruxelles: Latomus, 1984).

the soul, and, under the proper conditions, can foretell the future.
Quintus notes, ". . . how great is the power of the soul when it is
divorced from the bodily senses, as it is especially in sleep, and in
times of frenzy or inspiration "(*Div.* 1.57.129).

While the power of divination may be considered a natural power of
the soul, it is the result of the soul's divine origin. It is present
because of the divine nature, and Quintus sometimes says it is "infused
into [the soul] from without, and made a part of it by the will of God"
(*Div.* 1.31.66); or that, "it must be ascribed to divine Nature, from
which, . . . our souls have been drawn and poured forth" (*Div.*
1.49.110). Human souls are sprung from the divine soul, and since
their source and origin is in the divine soul, they are able to participate
in the divine knowledge of the future (*Div.* 1.32.70, 1.49.110).

Divine knowledge comes about, therefore, because of this divine
connection. It is by interconnection with the divine mind and the
divine souls which pervade the universe that souls, themselves of divine
origin, know the future. Quintus says, "And since the universe is
wholly filled with the Eternal Intelligence and the divine Mind, it must
be that human souls are influenced by their contact with divine souls"
(*Div.* 1.49.110). Quintus cites Posidonius' three ways of divine
knowledge, all of which depend upon the contact of the soul with the
divine:

> First, the soul is clairvoyant of itself because of its kinship
> with the gods; second, the air is full of immortal souls, already
> clearly stamped, as it were, with the marks of truth; and third,
> the gods in person converse with men when they are asleep.[13]

The natural power of divination and contact with the divine, however,
can only be exercised when the soul is freed from the influences of the
body. Like Plato, the tradition represented by Quintus holds that true
divine knowledge is frustrated by the body, and only occurs under those
circumstances when the influences of the body are restricted. According
to Quintus, there are two types of natural divination, that which occurs
in frenzy (*furor*), and that in dreams. In both circumstances, the soul

---

[13]*Div.* 1.30.64.

withdraws from the body. Frenzy itself is the separation of the soul from the body, when souls "spurning their bodies, take wings and fly abroad" (*Div.* 1.50.114). Quintus says, "If that power [divination] is abnormally developed, it is called 'frenzy' or 'inspiration,' which occurs when the soul withdraws itself from the body and is violently stimulated by a divine impulse" (*Div.* 1.31.66). In dreams, the body is restrained by sleep, and the soul is free to roam and converse with the divine souls around it. "When men are awake," says Quintus, "their souls, as a rule, are subject to the demands of every day life and are withdrawn from divine association because they are hampered by chains" (*Div.* 1.49.110). However, "while we sleep and the body lies as if dead, the soul is at its best, because it then is freed from the influence of the physical senses and from the worldly cares that weigh it down" (*Div.* 1.51.115). This is why the general public does not prophesy more; they are too embroiled in daily affairs to free the soul, and only those few who have cultivated the separation of body and soul are true seers. "In fact," he says, "the human soul never divines naturally, except when it is so unrestrained and free that it has absolutely no association with the body, as happens in the case of frenzy and dreams" (*Div.* 1.49.113).

Inspiration itself is described as a motion of the soul. The soul is moved, stirred, incited, or aroused into reaching for knowledge of the future. The natural ability of the soul, freed by separation from the body, is inspired to action by some stirring impulse. Quintus describes it as arousal, inflammation, excitement, and exaltation.[14] This excitement is due to a number of causes. According to Quintus, the soul is sometimes moved by divine impulse, which comes from God, and is external to the soul.[15] It occurs, he says, "when the soul

---

[14]*Div.* 1.18.34, concitatione; *Div.* 1.36.80, pellantur animi vehementius; *Div.* 1.40.89, mentis incitatione et permotione divina; *Div.* 1.50.114, ardore aliquo inflammati atque incitati.

[15]Wesley D. Smith has argued that the ancient model of inspiration was founded not on possession or ecstasy, but on the external incitation of the mantic soul. He argues that in Cicero, Plutarch and others, the prophet is not entered and possessed by divinity, but is influenced from outside the soul. He cites the well-known vapors at Delphi as an example. This is indeed the case with Cicero. Wesley D. Smith, "So-called Possession in Pre-Christian Greece," *Transactions*

withdraws itself from the body and is violently stimulated by a divine impulse (cum a corpore animus abstractus divino instinctu concitatur)."[16] As we have indicated, Quintus, citing Posidonius, says that the divine impulse (deorum appulsus) can come either from the immortal souls inhabiting the air, or from the gods in person while the body is asleep. The soul, however, may be moved by other influences. Quintus says,

> It often happens too, that the soul is violently stirred by the sight of some object, or by the deep tones of a voice, or by singing. Frequently anxiety or fear will have that effect.[17]

Strong emotion or passion is sufficient to incite the soul to prophecy, when it is in the proper condition. In dealing with oracular prophecy, Quintus also acknowledges that the soul can be moved by exhalations of the earth, such as occur at Delphi.[18] The gods not only impart their power to human beings, he says, but have enclosed it in caverns and various types of soils (*Div.* 1.36.79).

The frenzied soul, incited to motion by various influences, is not always trustworthy, however, and Quintus admits that there is room for error, particularly in dreams. Dreams can be troubled and confused, and the motion of the soul disturbed. The culprit is the body, especially when it is itself troubled by food and drink. Quintus says, " . . .when we are burdened with food and drink our dreams are troubled and confused."[19] He asserts, quoting Plato, that the Pythagoreans were forbidden to eat beans because "that food produces great flatulence and induces a condition at war with a soul in search of truth" (*Div.* 1.30.62). Presumably the *inflatio* of the beans interfered with the divine *inflatus* of inspired sleep.

---

and Proceedings of the American Philological Association 96 (1965):403-426. See also Aune, *Prophecy*, p. 33.

[16]*Div.* 1.31.66.

[17]*Div.* 1.36.80.

[18]Like Plutarch (*De def. or.* 434 A), Cicero offers this as an explanation of the lapse of the Delphic Oracle. *Div.* 1.19.38.

[19]*Div.* 1.29.61. Quintus quotes Plato's treatment of dreams in book 9 of the *Republic*.

It essential therefore, that the soul be prepared for untroubled prophecy. If one wishes prophetic dreams, food and drink before sleep must be restricted. Beyond that, the body itself must be regulated with a restrained diet, "so that the soul is in a condition to watch while the body sleeps" (*Div.* 1.51.115). To be a true seer, one must belong to that "certain class of men, though small in number, who withdraw themselves from carnal influences and are wholly possessed by an ardent concern for the contemplation of things divine" (*Div.* 1.49.111). The soul must be prepared by a regulation of the body and a restriction of its confusing and perverting influences on the prophetic powers of the soul.

Cicero's presentation of the pro-divination position provides a significant background for later discussions of prophecy. Like Plato, the position represented by Quintus affirms that natural divination, or prophecy, takes place in the soul as it is in contact with the divine. The soul is incited, or stirred to exercise its divine powers of prophecy, but this prophetic excitement is subject to perverting and confusing influences which make some of its experiences untrustworthy. For Quintus, as for Plato, these perverting influences come primarily from the body and its appetites. The external influences which stir the soul, however, suggest the possibility of other forces which might confuse and mislead the prophesying soul. In any case, it is training of the body, and regulation of the soul which overcome perverting influences and produce the true seer.

Plutarch. Plutarch, concerned as he is with the fortunes of the official oracle at Delphi, provides a wide-ranging discussion of the nature and causes of prophecy and inspiration, as well as its dangers and defects. His work manifests many of the same concerns as that of Cicero, and thus indicates a common scope of discussion concerning prophecy. Like Quintus in Cicero's dialogue, Plutarch deals with the prophetic powers inherent in the soul, their cultivation, and their potential for error. He likewise deals with the external forces which incite the soul to prophesy. Unlike Quintus, he places the responsibility for prophecy and inspiration with souls midway between the intelligible and sensible worlds, that is, the daemons.

Like Cicero, Plutarch affirms that the prophetic power is inherent in the soul. It is present in varying degrees in souls at all levels of purification, but in most souls joined to bodies it is weak to the point of being imperceptible. He says it is "about as ineffectual and slow in operation as persons that try to see in a fog" (*De def. or.* 431 F). Like memory, it is the ability to represent in image things which are not present, an ability exercised by memory on things past, by prophecy on things future (*De def. or.* 432 A). Plutarch places this power, as Plato does, in the irrational soul. Its fundamental function is to receive impressions which are made upon it, and Plutarch says it is "like a tablet without writing" (*De def. or.* 432 D).

Inspiration and prophecy for Plutarch, then, deal primarily in visions, images, and representations which are impressed upon the reflective quality of the prophetic power of the soul. These are φαντασίαι, visions or images which are produced in the soul. Plutarch does not regard inspiration as possession, but rather as this external stimulation of visions.[20] He says that the prophetic power (τὸ μαντικὸν) is a blank slate, "receptive of impressions (φαντασιῶν) through what may be done to it" (*De def. or.* 432 D). This is the line he takes in defending the crudity of the verses of the Pythia. The poetry belongs to the woman, not the god; the god is only responsible for the content of the oracle. He says, "As a matter of fact, the voice is not that of a god, nor the utterance of it, . . . but all these are the woman's; he puts into her mind only the visions, and creates a light in her soul in regard to the future; for inspiration is precisely this" (*De Pyth. or.* 397 C). Inspiration consists of the guidance and instruction of the soul by an external force. According to Plutarch, it is in this manner that Socrates' daemon guided him; he says, "It cannot be hard, I think, to believe that the understanding may be guided by a higher understanding and a diviner soul, that lays hold of it from without by a touch, which is the way in which it is the nature of thought to impinge on thought, just as light produces a reflection" (*De gen.* 589 B). Plutarch uses the *topos* of instrument and plectrum to describe inspiration; the soul is the

---

[20]Against the notion of prophetic possession, Plutarch has Lamprias say, "Certainly it is foolish and childish in the extreme to imagine that the god himself after the manner of ventriloquists (ἐγγαστρίμυθους) . . . enters into the bodies of his prophets and prompts their utterances, employing their mouths and voices as instruments." *De def. or.* 414 E. See Smith, "So-called Possession," p. 415.

instrument, while the inspiring force is the plectrum which moves the passive soul to reflect its φαντασίαι.[21]

The participants in Plutarch's dialogue *On the Obsolescence of Oracles* discuss several possibilities for the source of the external inspiring power. Plutarch, dealing with the lapse of the traditional oracles, considers the possibility, affirmed by Quintus, that the source of this external influence is gases or exhalations produced by various parts of the earth, and in particular, the grotto at Delphi. Plutarch notes that the earth produces exhalations of all kinds, some of which produce diseases and disorders of the soul, and asserts that the prophetic spirit (τὸ μαντικὸν ῥεῦμα καὶ πνεῦμα) is likewise an exhalation, which comes either through the air or in running water (*De def. or.* 432 D). He cites the traditions concerning the discovery of the prophetic power of the Delphic site, and notes that oracles come and go with the fluctuations of nature, and are affected quite often by the weather (*De def. or.* 434 C).

He is not content, however, to leave prophecy in the hands of nature. While inspiration may be considered to derive from terrestrial exhalations, prophecy is much more personally and divinely produced. It is the daemons who are responsible for the inspiration at the oracle sites, and for the moving of the souls of inspired persons. Plutarch takes the middle position on the question of the inspiration of the oracles; he affirms both that the inspiration comes from earthly gases, and that the daemons are the overseers of the exhalations, governing their output, and using them as instruments for carrying out inspiration as they desire. He says, "we leave demigods (δαίμονων) as overseers, watchmen, and guardians of this tempered constitution, as if it were a kind of harmony slackening here and tightening here on occasion."[22]

---

[21]*De def. or.* 436 F. Plutarch rejects the use of the lyre and plectrum image with regard to the prophetic experience as a whole. He feels it is appropriate, however, in discussing the production of images in the soul; like the strings of a lyre, the reflective powers of the prophetic faculty of the soul respond when plucked by some external force.

[22]*De def. or.* 437 A. Brenk argues that Plutarch's reference to the daemons here does not reflect his own position, but "seems more a polite concession to Cleombrotus than a serious modification or addition which has anything intrinsically to do with Lamprias' prophetic theory." *In Mist Apparelled*, p. 119.

Plutarch holds the Middle-Platonic view of the daemons as intermediaries between God and the affairs of humanity. They hold an intermediate position on the scale of the ascension of the soul, between the rank of hero and god, and are capable of rising or falling in virtue.[23] It is of them that the scurrilous events ascribed to the gods speak, and many of them are called by the name of the god with which they are associated.[24] They function as the intermediate agents of providence, connecting the mortal world with the divine, and carry out the mundane tasks which would not become the divine nature. They preside at religious ceremonies and, as the provincial agents of providence, are responsible for the variety of religious rites.[25]

More importantly, they carry out the task of inspiration. It is the daemons who, while also in charge of the oracle sites, bring about personal inspiration. It is the contact of soul with daemon that produces "impressions of the future" (φαντασίας τοῦ μέλλοντος, *De def. or.* 431 C). Daemons speak directly to the soul with "unuttered words," producing prophetic visions in individual souls (*De gen.* 588 D). This is particularly true in the context of the familiar daemon. Each soul, according to Plutarch, has its own assisting daemon, which guides and instructs it from birth to its ascension to the divine (*De gen.* 593 F). This daemon instructs the soul that is willing to listen, with

---

However, Lamprias argues very eloquently for the necessity of daemons, saying that both those who hold to a strictly theological position, and those espousing a material point of view are mistaken. "The one," he says, "ignores the intermediary and the agent, the other the source and the means." His concern is to maintain the action of providence in prophecy, and the daemons are essential to this.

[23] *De def. or.* 416 D, 415 C; *De Is. et Os.* 361 E. Cleombrotus' statements concerning the intermediate nature of the daemons probably represents the position of Xenocrates (*De def. or.* 416 D), while Plutarch himself considers the daemons to have a dynamic nature, capable of ascent or descent. John Dillon, *The Middle Platonists* (Ithaca: Cornell University Press, 1977), p. 32, 46. Brenk argues that for Plutarch, daemons are nothing more than human souls, and that in fact the activity of daemons is of little interest to Plutarch. Brenk, *In Mist Apparelled*, p. 111.

[24] According to Cleombrotus, *De def. or.* 417 E, 421 E. Brenk says that Plutarch later rejected the daemonological explanation of the myths in favor of the allegorical. Brenk, *In Mist Apparelled*, p. 102.

[25] *De def. or.* 417 A, *De Is. et Os.* 378 A.

thoughts and images which appear in the reflecting power of the soul. Socrates and his daemon are the best example, and in his dialogue *On the Daemon of Socrates* Plutarch indicates that the omens which guided Socrates, such as the famous sneeze, were the result of his personal daemon, which guided him in more intimate ways as well. He says,

> Socrates on the other hand, had an understanding which, . . . was so sensitive and delicate as to respond at once to what reached him. What reached him, one would conjecture, was not spoken language, but the unuttered words of a daemon, making voiceless contact with his intelligence by their sense alone.[26]

The myth in *On the Daemon of Socrates* indicates that the assisting daemon is actually a part of the soul. It is, however, that part of the soul which has never become immersed in the body. Timarchus is told, "This is not dragged in with the rest, but is like a buoy attached to the top, floating on the surface in contact with the man's head, while he is as it were submerged in the depths"(*De gen.* 591 E). Plutarch makes it clear, however, that this buoy is external, and so is properly called a daemon.[27] A daemon therefore is a soul or that part of the soul which is not involved with the body, and is attached to a human being, attempting to persuade it to rise above the material. Prophetic knowledge results from contact between this daemon who has knowledge of the future, and the human *nous*. Plutarch tells of daemons who, while their client souls are asleep, roam into the future, and return to report what they saw (*De gen.* 592 D). Inspired souls are those which obey their daemons.

---

[26]*De gen.* 588 D.

[27]Brenk emphasizes the humanity of the daemons, and argues that, since a daemon is a human soul, they have little significance in Plutarch's thought. Plutarch, however, makes it clear that, while daemons are souls, they are external to human beings, and exercise care and guidance over their human wards. Boyancé notes the ambiguity in the doctrine of the familiar daemon: "les rapports du démon personnel et de l'âme restent toujours à la fois très imprécis et très étroits; ils sont toujours plus ou moins identiques et plus ou moins différents." Pierre Boyancé, "Les deux démons personnels dans l'antiquité Grecque et Latine," *Revue de philologie de littérature et d'histoire anciennes* 3rd series, 9 (1935):192.

There are, however, both wicked daemons and unprepared souls, and consequently there can be error in prophecy. In *On the Obsolescence of Oracles* Cleombrotus, probably representing Xenocrates, speaks of wicked daemons who cause pestilence and war, and who must be appeased with sacrifices and religious rites.[28] Plutarch says that souls themselves, however, are rarely disciplined in such a way as to perceive the guidance of their daemons, and this can result in untrustworthy prophecies. He says,

> Whenever, then, the imaginative and prophetic faculty is in a state of proper adjustment for attempering itself to the spirit as to a drug, inspiration in those who foretell the future is bound to come; and whenever the conditions are not thus it is bound not to come, or when it does come to be misleading, abnormal, and confusing.[29]

It is in the prepared soul that inspiration takes place. The messages of the daemons come to many, but "find an echo in those only whose character is untroubled and soul unruffled" (*De gen.* 589 D). The soul must be withdrawn from the influences of the body, and the prophetic faculty must be free from the restraining caution of reason. This happens most often during sleep, but Plutarch says that there are those souls who by uncommon obedience and long discipline are attentive to their daemons even when awake. These are the best souls, chosen from humanity like a horse trainer chooses the best of the herd for his special attention. Plutarch says,

> so too our betters take the best of us, as from a herd, and setting a mark on us, honour us with a peculiar and exceptional schooling, guiding us not by rein or bridle, but by language

---

[28]*De def. or.* 417 D. See above, note 23.

[29]*De def. or.* 438 A. According to Brenk, Plutarch combines two Platonic strains: that requiring a certain temperament or *krasis*, and that requiring an inspiring *pneuma*. Brenk, *In Mist Apparelled*, p. 126.

expressed in symbols quite unknown to the generality and common herd of men.[30]

From these souls, he says, "which from their very beginning and birth are docile to the rein and obedient to their daemons, comes the race of diviners and men inspired" (*De gen.* 592 C).

Plutarch's dialogues on oracles and prophecy represent a wide spectrum of background and thought concerning such central topics in second-century discussion as the lapse of the traditional oracle sites and the nature of Socrates' daemon. Speaking from a Platonic context, but addressing many of the same issues as the Stoic tradition represented in Cicero's *On Divination*, they indicate that a common series of themes and areas of interest are present in the second-century background. Prophecy is held to be a faculty within the soul, which is primarily passive, and which reflects the stirrings or images presented from without. Particularly with Plutarch, inspiration consists of visions and intellectual images impressed upon the reflective powers of the soul. It is the daemonic realm which is responsible for this prophecy, and inspiration takes place by the guidance and communication of one's personal daemonic guide. It is only the disciplined soul, however, which can hear the promptings and reports of its daemon, and the soul is only able to perceive these external messages to the extent that it is withdrawn from the body and its influences. The important issues in dealing with true prophecy, then, are the state of the soul, its connection with the body, and the nature of the daemonic inspirer.

Philo. While Philo's interests in the matter of prophecy and inspiration are different from those of his non-Jewish contemporaries, he shares many of the same concerns in this area, and deals with the same issues, although in different ways. He addresses the nature of the soul and how it is moved to prophesy, the perverting influences and images which confuse it, and the necessity of the separation of the soul from the body.

Philo focuses on the soul and its experience of prophecy. In dealing with prophetic dreams, he, like Quintus, says that there are several

---

[30] *De gen.* 593 B.

ways in which the soul is moved to prophesy in dreams. In the first,
God himself moves the soul and provides prophetic suggestion. A
second kind of prophetic dream occurs when the soul stirs itself into
corybantic frenzy. The third type consists of the movement of the mind
in harmony with the Mind of the universe, producing possession,
inspiration, and divine madness (*Som.* 1.1, 2.1). This third type is
most characteristic of the prophet. For Philo, inspiration takes place
when the mind is severed from its earthly roots, and possessed by divine
frenzy (*Migr. Abr.* 190). This frenzy consists of a "heavenward
yearning,"[31] wherein the mind, breathed upon from above, is drawn
towards the divine *nous* and heavenly realities. The mind thus inspired
loses all restraint and possession of itself, and is truly possessed. Philo
says, "For it is the mind which is under the divine afflatus and no
longer in its own keeping, but is stirred to its depths and maddened by
heavenward yearning, drawn by the truly existent and pulled upward
thereto" (*Rer. div. her.* 69).

This raises the question of Philo's understanding of ecstasy. The
famous passage concerning ecstasy in *Who is the Heir* 264 seems to
indicate that Philo believes the prophetic experience to be one of
dispossession of human nature, and complete possession by the divine.
Indeed, he says, "The mind is evicted at the arrival of the divine
Spirit. . . . Mortal and immortal may not share the same home" (*Rer.
div. her.* 264). Dodds says of this passage, "This is not a description of
mystical union; what it describes is a state of 'temporary possession' or
what is nowadays called 'trance-mediumship.' "[32] However, it is
Philo's intention, at this point, to emphasize the divine aspect of
prophecy. He is asserting that the biblical writers contributed nothing
human to scripture, and that their prophecies are entirely of divine
origin. He says, "the prophet, even when he seems to be speaking,
really holds his peace, and his organs of speech, mouth and tongue, are
wholly in the employ of Another, to shew forth what He wills" (*Rer.
div. her.* 264).

In the context of his treatment of prophecy in *Who is the Heir*,
however, it is clear that Philo has more in mind than simple

---

[31]*Rer. div. her.* 69, ἔρωτι οὐρανίῳ.
[32]Dodds, *Pagan and Christian*, p. 72.

mediumship. The context of this passage itself indicates this. Philo begins by speaking of the mind; it is like the sun, illuminating the soul as the sun illuminates the earth. When the mind is functioning in this way, "we are self-contained, not possessed," says Philo; ἐν ἑαυτοῖς ὄντες οὐ κατεχόμεθα (Rer. div. her. 264). Possession, κατοκωχή, occurs when this light "sets," or the mind is removed from its illuminating and governing function. It is no longer "in itself." It is evicted (ἐξοικίζεται) and the divine spirit takes its place. In the darkness caused by the "setting" of reason, ecstasy and inspiration occur.[33]

Elsewhere Philo speaks of the condition of the mind when so possessed, or not "in itself." The mind in frenzy, "no longer in its own keeping (ἐνθουσιώσης γὰρ καὶ οὐκέτ᾽ οὔσης ἐν ἑαυτῇ διανοίας) . . . is stirred to its depths and maddened by heavenward yearning, drawn by the truly existent" (Rer. div. her. 69). The mind is drawn from its usual function and association with the body, and divorced from all concerns other than the upward call. It is outside even of itself, wrapped in frenzy and darkness. Philo's inspiration, then, is not simple mediumship, but a possession experience where the mind, particularly as reason, (διάνοια), is severed from its normal function as light of the soul and body and is wrapped in divine concerns.[34] The mind is no longer "in itself," but it is involved in the prophetic experience.[35]

---

[33]Rer. div. her. 265, διὰ τοῦτο ἡ δύσις τοῦ λογισμοῦ καὶ τὸ περὶ αὐτὸν σκότος ἔκστασιν καὶ θεοφόρητον μανίαν ἐγέννησε.

[34]Holladay, referring to Quaest. in Ex. 2.29, says that the soul of the prophet becomes unified into a completely rational state, but outside of corporeal existence. He says, "It is in this quintessential rational state that the prophetic nous is said to be 'immortal.' " Carl H. Holladay, Theios Aner in Hellenistic Judaism: A Critique of the Use of This Category in New Testament Christology, SBL Dissertation Series, no. 40 (Missoula, Montana: Scholars Press, 1977), pp. 159-160.

[35]Scholars have long debated whether the experiences which Philo describes represent the unio mystica of the mystic. Scholars like Danielou assert that the experience of the prophet is the final level of the mystic, the transformation from the "vie illuminative" to the "vie unitive," while Dodds argues the negative position. Holladay, however, correctly points out that distinctions between mysticism and prophecy are not helpful in regard to Philo: "the categories

The primary factor which can pervert and confuse this inspiration is the body and the sensible world, with its false images. The soul itself can be divided into upper and lower, rational and irrational, and it is the irrational soul which is identified with the senses and matter. The irrational soul, "like a torrent in five divisions pours through the channels of all the senses and rouses the violence of the passions" (*Fug.* 91). Like Quintus and Plutarch, Philo considers this influence to be reduced during sleep. Those dreams which occur when the dreamer is half awake, or just waking, are therefore less trustworthy, because the senses are beginning to regain their potency (*Som.* 2.18). The influence of the irrational and its material temptations produce false images in the mind, confusing and corrupting inspiration. Like most of his contemporaries, Philo views inspiration in terms of vision. The confusing power of the body produces false visions in the mind, which frustrate its ascent. Folly, says Philo, "robs the mind of true apprehensions, and fills it with false phantoms and untrustworthy visions (ψευδῶν δε εἰδώλων καὶ ἀβεβαίων φαντασμάτων, *Som.* 2.162)." The wicked attempt to bring the virtuous down into the realm of the impious, where there are "innumerable tribes of spectres and phantoms and dream-illusions (εἰδώλων καὶ φασμάτων καὶ ὀνειράτων ἔθνη μυρία, *Som.* 2.133)," while the righteous soul of Jacob was "full of real things, not of dreams and empty phantoms (ὀνειράτων καὶ κενῶν φαντασμάτων, *Fug.* 143)." The sensible world only produces "dreams and phantoms (τὰ ὀνείρατα καὶ φαντάσματα) of things that have the name and appearance of good things" (*Fug.* 129).

Only when the mind is completely separated from the irrational soul and the senses, then, can true and trustworthy inspiration take place. This can occur in deep sleep, as Philo says,

> In deep sleep the mind quits its place, and, withdrawing from
> the perceptions and all the other bodily faculties, begins to

---

'prophecy' and 'mysticism' as representing the two sides of the same coin, or even one side of a single coin, are artificial to the extent that they blur the basic fact that what really is under consideration is the two-directional event of revelation, or illumination, depending on one's vantage point." Jean Danielou, *Philon d'*

hold converse with itself, fixing its gaze on truth as on a mirror, and, having purged away as defilements all the impressions made upon it by the mental pictures presented by the senses, it is filled with Divine frenzy.[36]

The pure mind, the mind which has gone beyond the world of sense, and separated itself from its influence, is able to participate in inspiration. "One alone," says Philo, "is held worthy of [divine things], the recipient of inspiration from above . . . the wholly purified mind which disregards not only the body, but that other section of the soul which is devoid of reason" (Rer. div. her. 64).

According to Philo, this is the mind of the sage. He says, "no worthless person is God-inspired (ἐνθουσία) in the proper sense. The name only befits the wise (μόνῳ δὲ σοφῷ, Rer. div. her. 259)." These are the ones who have successfully undertaken the life of progress from sensible things to intelligible, and have consequently risen above the confusing influences of things below. The soul that inherits divine things, says Philo, has left the body, the senses, and even itself, and is, as we have seen, "no longer in its own keeping (ἐν ἑαυτῇ, Rer. div. her. 69)." The mind in this condition is guarded by its divine inspiration from any further perverting influence, and the sage thus stands above the instability of mortal life. For Philo, the sage stands midway between humanity and God, "bounded at either end . . . by mortality because of manhood, by incorruption because of his virtue" (Som. 2.229). According to Philo, the soul of the sage is a heaven on earth, and his mind is "released from storms and wars, with calm, still weather and profound peace around it."[37] Philo's concerns are similar to those of his contemporaries. In dealing with prophecy, of primary importance is the state of the soul and its relationship to hindering influences of the body and the corporeal world.

Alexandrie (Paris:Librairie Artheme Fayard, 1958), p. 193; Dodds, Pagan and Christian, p. 78; Holladay, Theios Aner, p. 164.

[36] Rer. div. her. 64.

[37] Som. 2.229. Holladay argues that Philo's fundamental apologetic concern is to credit the Hebrew leaders with all the Stoic virtues, and to portray Moses as the Cynic-Stoic σοφός βασιλεύς. Holladay, Theios Aner, p. 112.

This survey has shown that there are certain key areas in the hellenistic discussion of prophecy. With Philo, as with the other representatives of the Greek background we have examined, primary attention is given to the soul of the prophet and to its condition during the prophetic experience. While understandings of the nature of inspiration have varied, the basic concern remains the same. The soul, in inspiration, is moved to see the eternal realities. This motion, however, can only be accomplished with proper preparation: the soul must be removed from influences which can confuse and pervert the prophetic vision. Vision is, indeed, the primary image in this discussion. The soul experiences images and visions as it reflects the divine inspiration, but other forces, external and internal, also produce false images which can mislead the soul. Φαντασίαι and φάσματα may appear from the bodily passions or wicked souls and cloud the clear sight of prophecy. This theoretical treatment of prophecy and inspiration lays the groundwork for polemical discussion about the true and false prophet. The central issues will be the nature of the soul of the sage and its associations, and whether the sage is far enough removed from evil influences to prophesy in a trustworthy way.

APOLOGETIC CONTEXT

Prophecy and inspiration present a field ripe for apologetic and polemic. The various philosophical schools carried on debate over the validity and nature of prophecy and divination, while in the more popular literature of satire and novel, various figures were either praised or lampooned as divine men and prophets.[38] Much of this polemic is

---

[38]The term *divine man* is used in a broad and non-specific sense to denote extraordinary, wonder-working figures. Modern criticism of the history of religions use of this term has questioned the identification of the divine man as a specific type, and indicated the wide scope of the term's meaning. See Ludwig Bieler, *Theios Aner: Das Bild des gottlichen Menschen in Spätantike und Frühchristentum* (Darmstadt: Wissenschaftliche Buchgesellschaft, 1976, 1st published 1935-1936); David L. Tiede, *The Charismatic Figure as Miracle Worker*; Morton Smith, "On the History of the Divine Man;" Eugene V. Gallagher, *Divine Man or Magician?*

carried on in the characterizations of divine men, as their followers sing their virtues, and their opponents denounce them as sorcerers. Prophecy is a vital part of this debate, because divine foreknowledge is a necessary characteristic of the divine man, while divination by the black art is a feature of the sorcerer.[39] With figures such as Moses and Apollonius, proponents and opponents examine their character to determine the nature of their inspiration and divination. In these debates several themes emerge which provide a background for the polemic of Origen and Celsus. For the critics, there are skeptical arguments against prophecy in general, but also attacks on the ambiguity of the opponent's prophecy, charges of sorcery, and the issue of phantoms and apparitions. For the defenders of specific prophets, the clarity of their visions, the virtue of their lives and discipline, the power they exercise over intervening influences, and the pure and divine nature of their souls provide the weapons of defense.

Polemic against Prophecy. Cicero, representing the New Academy, presents skeptical arguments against the very existence of divination. Concerning the oracles collected by the Stoics he says, "of these some, as I think, were false; some came true by chance, as happens very often even in ordinary speech; and are some so equivocal that they require a dialectician to construe them" (*Div.* 2.55.115). For him, the reputation of divination rests simply upon chance, which is the only thing that accounts for the fulfillment of oracles; or upon their ambiguity, which makes it impossible to tell whether they have been fulfilled or not. With respect to chance, the skeptic in Plutarch's dialogue argues that fulfillment cannot be a proof for divination, because over an eternity of time, chance brings everything to pass. While an oracle may eventually be fulfilled, at the time it is uttered it is a lie. "The telling of things non-existent," he says, "contains error in itself" (Plutarch *De Pyth. or.* 399 A).

Beyond the skeptical arguments against the validity of divination in general, the argument from the ambiguity of the prophecy under attack is a central one in this debate. The dark and obscure oracle had a long and respected tradition, but the obscure oracle in the second century,

---

[39]See Harold Remus, *Pagan and Christian Conflict.*

particularly as used by wandering prophets and divine men, raised questions among their critics. Cicero argues that it is unfitting for the gods to send unintelligible communications, (Cicero *Div.* 2.64.132) while Plutarch notes that in the past, obscurity was a sign of divine power, but that lately, people, "were coming to look with suspicion upon metaphors, riddles, and ambiguous statements, feeling that these were secluded nooks of refuge devised for furtive withdrawal and retreat for him that should err in his prophecy" (Plutarch *De Pyth. or.* 407 A). Lucian, in his caricature of Alexander, says that Alexander gave oracles that were "sometimes obscure and ambiguous, sometimes downright unintelligible, for this seemed to him in the oracular manner" (Lucian *Alex.* 22). For Lucian, however, the ambiguity served both to 'con' the crowds, and cover Alexander's deceptions. The responses of Alexander were more ambiguous the more carefully the scrolls containing the questions were sealed. Ambiguity is a sign of quackery, for Lucian; Cocconas, Alexander's partner in dreaming up the con game, made his living composing "equivocal, ambiguous, obscure oracles" (*Alex.* 10). For those who believe in prophecy, however, ambiguity is a sign of improper preparation of the soul, and the intervention of inimical influences, often those of the body. Apollonius, in defense of his austere diet and abstention from wine, argues that the soul which goes to sleep drunk is bound to have obscured dreams. Dream interpreters, he says, refuse to interpret dreams which take place before midnight, "when the soul is immersed in the lees of wine and muddied thereby" (Philostratus *VA* 2.37). Prophecies which are confused and ambiguous, then, are either the result of fraud and deception, or the product of an impure soul, and are untrustworthy.

An equally significant attack on the prophet and his inspiration is the charge of sorcery. This charge accompanies all the claimants to the divine man status, and much of the debate around these figures centers on the issue of whether they are θεῖοι or γόητες.[40] In connection with prophecy, this polemic deals with whether the prophecies are indeed the result of divine association or the manipulations of a

---

[40] See Remus, *Pagan and Christian Conflict,* and Peter Brown, "Sorcery, Demons, and the Rise of Christian Conflict from Late Antiquity into the Middle Ages," in Mary Douglas, ed., *Witchcraft Confessions and Accusations,* A.S.A. Monographs, no. 9 (London: Tavistock, 1970):17-45.

magician. For Lucian, sorcery is entirely an enterprise in trickery, and γοητεία is synonymous with fraud. A magician, in this case Alexander, deals in "clever schemes, bold emprises, and sleights of hand,"(*Alex.* 1) and Lucian's details on the tricks Alexander used to produce oracles are well-known. In other cases the issue is not so much that of fraud, but whether the prophet achieves his results by τέχνη or by divine association. According to Philostratus, some "would rob Apollonius of the credit of having predicted things by dint of wisdom (τὸ κατὰ σοφίαν προγιγνώσκειν), and say that he achieved these results by art of wizardry (ὡς μάγῳ τέχνῃ)" (Philostratus *VA* 1.2). The issue is whether the prophet has manufactured his oracles by the manipulation of charms or daemons, or whether his soul is sufficiently wise and pure to receive divine knowledge. Apollonius cites Pythagoras, Democritus, and Socrates as those who knew divine truth because of association with the divine, and "yet never stooped to τέχνη" (*VA* 1.2). Philo says equally of Moses that the wonders produced by God in Egypt finally caused his detractors to regard "these events not as the works of human cunning or artifices fabricated to deceive, but as brought about by some diviner power to which every feat is easy" (Philo *Vit. Mos.* 1.94).

Concomitant with the charge of sorcery is the discussion of apparitions. Apollonius frequently encountered them, demonstrated his power over them, and was charged with consorting with them as a part of his magical practices. Philostratus replies in defense that Apollonius made his prophecies "by some divine impulse," and was not a wizard. "Wizards," says Philostratus, " . . . claim to alter the course of destiny, by having recourse either to the torture of lost spirits, or to barbaric sacrifices" (Philostratus *VA* 5.12). Apollonius himself asserted that, like ambiguity, phantasms and apparitions appeared to souls not adequately prepared. Wine and sleeping drugs "drench the soul and body," and "cause the light and distracted sleep of men haunted by phantoms" (*VA* 2.36). Skeptics argued that the religious Platonism which relied upon prophecy and inspiration was characterized by association with apparitions. Galaxidorus, the critic in Plutarch's dialogue *On the Daemon of Socrates*, says that philosophy had been "left by Pythagoras and his company a prey of phantoms, fables and superstition (φασμάτων δὲ καὶ μύθων καὶ δεισιδαιμονίας, Plutarch *De gen.* 580 C)." According to Galaxidorus, those who claim "to be favorites of heaven and above the common sort . . . [hide] what occurs to their intelligence behind a pretense of dreams and apparitions (ὀνείρατα καὶ φάσματα) and the like mummery" (Plutarch *De gen.* 579 A). Lucian says that Alexander's burning of Epicurus' *Established Beliefs* occurred because the book liberates its readers "from terrors and apparitions and portents (δειμάτων καὶ φασμάτων καὶ τεράτων, Lucian *Alex.* 47)."

These charges are representative of the kind of polemic centering around prophecy and prophets. Arguments used to call the inspiration of prophets into question included attacks on the ambiguity and obscurity of their oracles; charges that they were sorcerers or quacks; and claims that the prophets, rather than dealing in clear truth, were actually involved with untrustworthy phantasms and apparitions.

Apologetic. Apologetic treatment of inspiration and the prophecy of the divine men attempted to show that their prophecy was not subject to such claims of ambiguity, sorcery, and dealings with phantoms. The defense naturally took the opposing position: the prophecies of the true divine men are clear and effective; the prophet stands well beyond the realm of sorcery; and he is unaffected by apparitions. In demonstrating these claims, apologetic focused on the soul of the prophet, emphasizing his preparation in virtue, his power over the intermediate world, and the ascent of his soul above those of others. The true prophet foretells the future by his contact with the divine.

If the mark of the charlatan is ambiguity, the mark of true prophecy is clarity. According to Iarchas, the Indian sage whom Apollonius meets, the true prophet, "with ever louder and clearer tone and truer import will . . . utter his oracles" (Philostratus *VA* 3.42). Philostratus demonstrates that such is the case with Apollonius. Asclepius himself refers a case to Apollonius, whose clear and unambiguous command to reform behavior and diet results in a cure. Philostratus compares this to Heraclitus, who dealt with the same affliction with a "very unintelligible remark . . . and by no means clear; but the sage [Apollonius] restored the youth to health by a clear interpretation of the wise saw" (*VA*) 1.9).

If the true prophet is able to see and prophesy clearly, he is also beyond the influence and deception of apparitions and phantoms. Philostratus makes this clear in his portrayal of Apollonius. In his travels Apollonius encounters several apparitions and, unlike ordinary folk, is able to discern the phantom and chase it off. Near the Indus,

Philostratus tells us, the φάσμα of a goblin appeared to Apollonius and his party, shifting and changing forms. Apollonius, undaunted, insulted it and it fled (*VA* 2.4). Likewise, on his trip to the springs of the Nile Apollonius was able to purge a village that had been troubled by an apparition for ten months (*VA* 6.27). Ephesus as well had been struck by a plague, and only Apollonius was able to discern that a certain beggar was actually a φάσμα who was causing the plague (*VA* 4.10). Apollonius, in his defense to Thespesion, says that this faculty of discernment and the power over apparitions were gifts from Wisdom, coming as a consequence of purity. Wisdom said to him,

> And when you are pure I will grant you the faculty of foreknowledge, and I will so fill your eyes with light, that you shall distinguish a god, and recognize a hero, and detect and put to shame the shadowy phantoms which disguise themselves in the form of men.[41]

As a prophet, Apollonius is able to see clearly into all levels of reality, and discern truth which eludes ordinary people.

As Apollonius says, this faculty comes as a result of purity, and the primary way the apologists refute the charges of sorcery and deception is with an examination of the lives and discipline of the prophets. This is true in the case of Apollonius, and in Philo's description of Moses as well. Apollonius, we are told, early dedicated himself to the Pythagorean lifestyle,[42] and continued throughout his life to exercise a discipline which resulted in his prophetic powers. In his defense speech before Domitian, Apollonius attributes much of his spiritual vision to his diet. He says, "This diet, my king, guards my senses in a kind of indescribable ether or clear air, and forbids them to contract any foul or turbid matter, and allows me to discern as in the sheen of a looking-

---

[41]Philostratus *VA* 6.11, ὡς διαγιγνώσκειν μὲν θεόν, γιγνώσκειν δὲ ἥρωα, σκιοειδῆ δ᾽ ἐλέγχειν φαντάσματα, ὅτε ψεύδοιντο εἴδη ἀνθρώπων.

[42]Philostratus *VA* 1.7. Philostratus indicates that this is the result of divine election. He intends the entire life of Apollonius, from miraculous birth to post mortem appearances, to indicate his divine status. On Apollonius' Pythagorean lifestyle, see Rudolf Arbesmann, "Fasting and Prophecy in Pagan and Christian Antiquity," *Traditio* 7 (1949-1951):27-30.

glass, everything that is happening or is to be" (*VA* 8.7). He explains his ability to discern the cause of the Egyptian pestilence by his "lighter diet" (*VA* 8.5). Preparation for prophetic dreams in sleep includes an austere diet before bed, abstinence from wine, and sleeping in garments made from non-animal materials. Of linen, Apollonius says, "It is a pure substance under which to sleep of a night, for to those who live as I do dreams bring the truest of revelations" (*VA* 8.7). The abstention from animal garments and food is extended to animal sacrifices as well, which, as Philostratus makes clear, indicates how Apollonius rises above sorcerers or even ordinary diviners. Apollonius says,

> But to what a depth of folly and inconsequence should I have descended if, after talking so much about divination and about the conditions under which it flourishes or does not flourish, I, who understand better than anyone that the gods reveal intentions to holy and wise men even without their possessing prophetic gifts, made myself guilty of bloodshed, by meddling with entrails of victims, as unacceptable to myself as they are ill-omened? In that case the revelation of heaven would surely have abandoned me as impure.[43]

His prophecy is thus due to his purity. Iarchas, the Indian sage, perceives that Apollonius' soul is filled with ether and thus he knows that he has foreknowledge. He says,

> Consequently I consider that one who would foresee events must be healthy in himself, and must not have his soul stained with any sort of defilement nor his character scarred with the wounds of any sins; so he will pronounce his predictions with purity, because he will understand himself and the sacred tripod in his breast.[44]

According to Philo, Moses also was remarkable for his discipline. Like Apollonius, as a teenager he disciplined and tamed the raging

---

[43]Philostratus *VA* 8.7.
[44]Philostratus *VA* 3.42.

passions of adolescence (Philo *Vit. Mos.* 1.25). His sojourn in Arabia was spent "carrying out the exercises of virtue with an admirable trainer, the reason within him, under whose discipline he laboured to fit himself for life in its forms, the theoretical and practical" (*Vit. Mos.* 1.48). In his priestly function he maintained purity, abstaining from women. According to Philo, this purity and discipline was necessary for his prophetic office. Moses practiced chastity, "almost from the time when, possessed by the spirit, he entered on his work as prophet, since he held it fitting to hold himself always in readiness to receive the oracular messages."[45]

For apologetic writers, then, concerned with promoting and defending the prophetic abilities of their heroes, purity guarantees their prophetic claims. The apologetic concern is to demonstrate not so much that the prophet has mantic abilities, but that he is a sage, and possesses divine knowledge because of his association with God. The soul of the prophet has succeeded in ascending above all the limiting influences of flesh and the world to achieve knowledge of true reality and the future.

Philo exemplifies this in his treatment of the prophetic soul. As we have seen, he argues that the mind of the sage is midway between the human and divine, "released from storms and wars, with calm still weather and profound peace around it . . . superior to men but less than God" (Philo *Som.* 2.229). The soul of the sage is the counterpart of heaven on earth, marked by its divine order and harmony, "revolving as God directs rays of virtues, supremely starlike and dazzling" (Philo *Rer. div. her.* 88). Moses is portrayed as an example of this nature. Philo says that those who saw him were amazed and "considered earnestly what the mind which dwelt in his body like an image in its shrine could be, whether it was human or divine or a mixture of both, so utterly unlike was it to the majority, soaring above them and exalted to a grander height" (Philo *Vit. Mos.* 1.27). According to Philo, Moses had his divine abilities because of his association with God: "if . . . what belongs to friends is common, and the prophet is called the friend of

---

[45] Philo *Vit. Mos.* 2.67. Holladay shows that Philo's concern in all of the three offices of Moses, those of prophet, priest, and king, is to emphasize the ethical quality of his character, and to paint him as the fulfillment of all of the Stoic virtues. Holladay, *Theios Aner*, p. 194.

God, it would follow that he shares also God's possessions" (*Vit. Mos.*
1.156).

Philostratus draws the same picture of the soul of Apollonius. In his
defense before Tigellinus, Apollonius, accused of sorcery, is asked to
prophesy on demand. Philostratus reports,

> 'How,' said Apollonius, 'can I, being no prophet (μάντις)?
> . . . Quite true is what you heard; but you must not put this
> down to any prophetic gift (μαντικῇ), but rather to the wisdom
> which God reveals to wise men.'[46]

Apollonius is not a diviner, but a sage. Apollonius tells us that "the
gods reveal their intentions to holy and wise men even without their
possessing prophetic gifts (μὴ μαντευομένοις φαίνουσι,
Philostratus *VA* 8.7)." Philostratus, like Philo, portrays his sage as
having ascended above the ordinary class of men, and attained a level
midway between God and man. Unlike most diviners, he says,
Apollonius does not need to wait for terrestrial exhalations to know the
future:

> he will notice these things when they are impending, not so
> soon indeed as the gods, yet sooner than the many. For the
> gods perceive what lies in the future, and men what is going on
> before them, and wise men what is approaching.[47]

According to Philostratus, the sage transcends "all things upon earth,"
and approaches the gods (*VA* 1.5). The true prophet prophesies neither
by skill nor art, but by the ascension of his soul to the divine,
accomplished by discipline of body and soul, and by his success in
overcoming the hindering influences of the body and the material world.

---

[46]Philostratus *VA* 4.44.
[47]Ibid.

Conclusion. This survey of the hellenistic background indicates the sort of context in which the polemic of pagan and Christian concerning prophecy appeared. As we have seen, while particular understandings of prophecy and inspiration have varied, a series of basic issues are central in the second-century discussion of prophecy. First of all, the fundamental question of how inspiration takes place centers around the issue of the motion of the soul. Prophecy is criticized and defended on the basis of the stirring of the prophetic abilities of the soul, either by internal or external forces. Second, bound up in this is the issue of the nature of those forces which affect the perception of the soul. Questions are raised concerning the effects of the body, of external divine and daemonic powers, and of wicked souls. Third, all of these forces produce images and phantasms, and apologetic effort is exerted to remove the prophet from the realm of false φάσματα, φαντασίαι, and the ambiguity produced by the forces hindering inspiration. The most important issue, therefore, is that of the state of the soul of the prophet. To evade the hindering influences, it must be trained by long discipline, and elevated by a pure life. Critiques of prophecy focus on the wicked soul of the charlatan, while the chief apologetic point to be won is that the prophet is much more than a *mantis*, and is indeed a sage, possessing divine knowledge by the elevation of his soul.

This emphasis on the nature of inspiration and prophecy fits into the development of Platonism in this period. Festugière has shown that contemporary views on knowledge of God focus on interior illumination and the regeneration of the pure soul. He argues convincingly that this is a development on the foundations of the Old Academy and Pythagoreanism, and polemic concerning prophecy fits well into this context.[48] Hans Lewy has noted this emphasis as well in the *Chaldean Oracles*. The *Chaldean Oracles* describe a system of divine knowledge in which the soul must purify itself for the ascension through the restraining powers of the wicked daemons to achieve mystical knowledge of God. Lewy describes the type of emphasis we have seen in the discussions of prophecy in this period:

---

[48] André Jean Festugière, *La révélation d'Hermès Trismégiste*, t. 1: *Le Dieu inconnu et la gnose* (Paris: Librairie Lecoffre, 1954), p. ix, 132.

the process of cognition was not regarded as an autonomous act of apprehension, but as the state of being filled with the divine light. . . . Human reason is transformed from an instrument of dialectical thinking, into the organ receiving the divine light, through which the noetic object is imparted to the purified soul. As we shall see, this mystical transfiguration of Plato's general doctrine of metaphysical cognition conforms to a general tendency characteristic of the Platonism of the period in which the Chaldaean Theurgists lived.[49]

The pagan and Christian discussion of prophecy stands firmly within this tradition.

---

[49]Hans Lewy, *The Chaldean Oracles and Theurgy*, ed. Michael Tardieu (Paris: Etudes Augustiniennes, 1978), p. 175.

Chapter 3

"Safe and Profitable:"

The Christian Background

> There existed, long before this time, certain
> men more ancient than all those who are
> esteemed philosophers, both righteous and
> beloved by God, who spoke by the Divine
> Spirit, and foretold events which would take
> place, and which are now taking place. They
> are called prophets. *Justin, Dial. 7.*

Justin Martyr's long search for truth among the philosophical schools
was at last consummated when he heard about certain men of old, who
"spoke those things which they saw and heard, being filled with the
Holy Spirit." "Straightway," he says, "a flame was kindled in my soul;
and a love of the prophets, and of those men who are friends of Christ,
possessed me." According to Justin, the prophets made him a true
philosopher and imparted that philosophy which alone was "safe and
profitable" (Justin *Dial.* 8). Such a conversion account is often repeated
throughout Christian apologetic. Tatian similarly credits the prophets
with his conversion, while Theophilus tells us that his journey to
belief was completed when he "met with the sacred Scriptures of the
holy prophets, who also by the Spirit of God foretold the things that
have already happened" (Theophilus *Auto.* 1.14). A reliance on
revelation and a "love for the prophets" stand at the center of second-
century Christian apologetic, and it is clear that the apologists consider
the argument from prophecy one of the most compelling in their

arsenal. The foundations for this reliance on the prophets are easily discernible. Nearly all the apologists cite two arguments: the prophets are true and inspired, first, because their teaching is a great deal older than that of the Greek sages, and second, because much of what they predicted has already come true. Plato borrowed from Moses, and the church stands as proof of prophetic accuracy.

The old man of Justin's conversion makes use of these well-known warrants, but also reveals that in Christian discussions of prophecy, particularly those of the apologists, more is at stake than the commonplaces of Christian rhetoric. He says that the prophets were worthy of credit because they glorified God and proclaimed the Christ, "which, indeed, the false prophets, who are filled with the lying unclean spirit, neither have done nor do, but venture to work certain wonderful deeds for the purpose of astonishing men, and glorify the spirits and demons of error" (Justin *Dial.* 7.3).

With this, the argument has gone beyond antiquity and fulfillment; the question here is one of spiritual deceit, power, and discernment. In the Christian literature which forms a background for the criticisms of Celsus and the reply of Origen, prophecy plays a central role in the conflict between the Greek and Christian worlds. As we have indicated, prophecy and inspiration had a long and (for the most part) respected tradition in the hellenistic world. The Christians, particularly the apologists, had to deal with this tradition in their own claims to divine truth. What results is a debate over the knowledge of God, the successful evasion of daemonic influence, and the locus of divine truth and power. For the Christians, the Greek world and its accomplishments lie under the deceiving power of the daemons, while divine truth is found only with those who have truly received it from God, through the prophets and Christ.

The background for the Christian side of this argument can be found in an examination of early Christian treatments of true and false prophecy, spiritual discernment, and knowledge of divine truth. The *Shepherd* of Hermas provides the early background for this issue, while apologists such as Justin, Tatian, Athenagoras, and Tertullian provide a direct background for the polemics of Celsus and Origen. In addition, the debate between Peter and Simon Magus in the Clementine literature gives a context of polemic which is perhaps similar to that provided by Lucian and the *Life of Apollonius* in the hellenistic world.

THE SHEPHERD

The *Shepherd* of Hermas, particularly its 11th Mandate, paints an intriguing picture of prophetic struggle.[1] Jannes Reiling has convincingly argued that Hermas is concerned with the intrusion of pagan divinatory practices into the prophecy of the church, and says, "The 11th Mandate has yielded the picture of a bitter conflict between Christian prophecy and hellenistic magic divination."[2] According to Reiling, the practice of giving oracles in private, prophesying for money, responding to inquiries, and telling inquirers what they wish to hear, all condemned in the 11th Mandate, indicate conflict between pagan and Christian forms of prophecy.[3] For Hermas, prophetic discernment involves a struggle between the holy spirit and the earthly spirit, with the souls of the double-minded as the prize.

Mandate 11 is devoted to the false prophet. This one, says Hermas, lacks the power provided by the divine spirit. Such a prophet is not merely a fraud, however; he is inspired by a false spirit which enables him to answer the oracular queries posed to him, and sometimes even to

---

[1] The authorship and date of the *Shepherd* are controverted. Many scholars see it as a composite work, involving several authors, with a final compilation made somewhere in the early second century. However, others, such as Robert Joly ("Hermas et le Pasteur," *Vigiliae Christianae* 21 (1967):201-208), have rejected a multiple authorship, and seen a single author, either writing the work completely at once, or in parts. Lage Pernveden sees value in attempting to find continuity in the *Shepherd* as a whole, since past research has proceeded with a critical approach to the text, neglecting the overall view. Lage Pernveden, *The Concept of the Church in the Shepherd of Hermas* (Lund: Gleerup, 1966), p. 14.

[2] Jannes Reiling, *Hermas and Christian Prophecy*, Supplements to *Novum Testamentum*, no.37 (Leiden: E. J. Brill, 1973), p. 47. Reiling notes that the word group *mantis* is used in early Christian literature before the apologists only here and in Acts (and in the LXX), and pagan divination is its intended target (p. 35).

[3] Ibid., p. 54. However, Aune questions the use of the charge of telling people what they wish to hear as a indication of Christian condemnation of false prophecy, on the basis that it was too widespread in antiquity. D. E. Aune, "*Herm. Man.* 11.2: Christian False Prophets Who Say What People Wish to Hear," *Journal of Biblical Literature* 97 (1978): 104.

speak the truth. This spirit is earthly, (ἐπίγειον), empty (κενόν), light (ἐλαφρόν), foolish (μωρόν), diabolic, and associated with idolatry. It is opposed by the holy spirit, and for Hermas, the conflict becomes obvious when the two spirits confront each other in the church. The shepherd says, "But when the false prophet comes into a meeting full of righteous men, who have a spirit of the Godhead, and intercession is made by them, that man is made empty, and the earthly spirit flees from him in fear, and that man is made dumb and is altogether broken up, being able to say nothing" (*Man.* 11.14). The conflict between true and false prophecy is thus a conflict between true, powerful inspiration on the one hand, and the false, empty inspiration of the devil, pagan practices, and idolatry, on the other.

The arena for this spiritual conflict is the soul of the double-minded. The false prophet's activity is to "corrupt the understanding of the servants of God;" but, says Hermas, "he corrupts the understanding of the double-minded, not of the faithful" (*Man.* 11.1). The double-minded approach him for oracles (ὡς ἐπὶ μάντιν), and he answers them "according to their wicked desires" (*Man.* 11.2). According to Hermas, the double-minded are constantly in flux, practice soothsaying, and, by association, idolatry (*Man.* 11.4). Like their prophet, they are empty, and receive empty oracles.

The sin of double-mindedness (διψυχία) plays a significant role in the *Shepherd*, and is closely linked to Hermas' anthropology, and thus to his understanding of what takes place in true and false prophecy. The double-minded are those who waver: they are uncertain concerning the truth (*Vis.* 3.4), are weak in confidence in the Lord (*Vis.* 4.2), hesitate in prayer (*Man.* 9.5), fail in any enterprise (*Man.* 10.2), are attracted to false prophets (*Man.* 11), are involved in worldly affairs (*Sim.* 8.8), and fall in the face of persecution.[4]

---

[4] See O.J.F. Seitz for the background of διψυχία in the Jewish-Christian tradition. O.J.F. Seitz, "Antecedents and Signification of the Term Δίψυχος," *Journal of Biblical Literature* 66 (1947):211-219; "Relationship of the Shepherd of Hermas to the Epistle of James," *Journal of Biblical Literature* 63 (1944):131-140; "Afterthoughts on the Term 'Dipsychos'," *New Testament Studies* 4 (1958):327-334. See also W. D. Davies, *Paul and Rabbinic Judaism* rev. ed. (New York: Harper, 1953), p. 20, and Jean Daniélou, *The Development of Christian Doctrine before the Council of Nicea*, vol. 1, *The Theology of Jewish*

Hermas fits this concept into a 'two-spirit' anthropology. The shepherd announces, "There are two angels with man, one of righteousness and one of wickedness" (*Man.* 6.2.1). The angel of righteousness works righteousness, resulting in sincerity, reverence, contentment, and virtue. However, when ill-temper, bitterness, and evil works arise, it is due to the effect of the evil angel. Human beings are thus not presented simply with two sets of actions, but with an inner warfare between two spirits, in which they must choose the side to which they will submit.[5] The servants of God are commanded to shun the evil spirit and put on the holy spirit, and people are bidden to submit themselves to the power of the righteous spirit, so that the power of the evil spirit might be conquered. For this purpose, Mandate 8 urges ἐγκράτεια, self-control. The evil spirit must be restrained and subdued, while the good spirit must be allowed free operation. Both sin and repentance involve the shedding of one power and the putting on of its opposite (*Sim.* 9.13).

It is in this context that the problem of double-mindedness, particularly with regard to the issue of prophecy, becomes clear. For Hermas, the two-spirit anthropology mandates purity. Righteousness is attained by complete association with the righteous spirit, while any flirtation with the evil spirit effectively quenches the work of the divine. Hermas says, "But if any ill-temper enters, the holy spirit, which is delicate, is discomforted immediately, and since it does not have a clean place, it seeks to leave the place. For it is choked by the evil spirit" (*Man.* 5.2). Believers are like jars of wine, says Hermas. The faithful are full of good wine, and the wine master does not worry about them. Jars partially full, however, soon turn sour, as the devil, unable to find room within those full of faith, enters those who are not full. The mixture of the two spirits within the same vessel results in the defilement of the righteous spirit, and the ultimate destruction of the vessel (*Man.* 12.5, 5.1). The double-minded, then, are those who are not completely full of the righteous spirit, who waver between the spirits, and attempt to mix them. This drives out the righteous spirit,

---

Christianity) trans. John A. Baker (London: Dartman, Longman, & Todd, 1964), p. 358.

[5] See Pemveden, *Church in the the Shepherd*, pp. 206-222.

and leaves the double-minded open to the work of the empty spirit, who occupies all unoccupied space. Spiritual power and victory depend upon purity, and thus the double-minded, mixed as they are, are conquered by the empty spirit and its prophet.

In the *Shepherd* of Hermas, the issue of inspiration and prophecy is set within a number of conflicts. Reiling has shown the dimension of conflict with pagan views of prophecy and divinatory practices, and Hermas reinforces this with his association of the false prophet and idolatry. Equally important is Hermas' portrayal of the spiritual conflict. The contest between true and false prophecy is intimately connected with the struggle of the spirits within the human being. Victory in the personal conflict is achieved by purity; the double-minded who waver and are mixed in spiritual allegiance are the victims. They are also the victims of false prophecy; they are open to the working of the false spirit, which cannot touch the righteous. The prophetic conflict, like the interior one, is one of power and impotence, fullness and emptiness, the spirit from above and the earthly spirit. In the milieu represented by Hermas, prophecy is at the heart of the issues of purity, righteousness, and spiritual power, and Hermas' work demonstrates the scope and significance of the debate over prophecy in the polemics of early Christianity.

THE APOLOGISTS.

The apologetic literature provides a somewhat different context for the discussion of prophecy and inspiration. It is explicit in the apologists' writing that the struggle between pagan and Christian is the conflict between the spirit of God and the spirit of this world. It is the apologist's task to demonstrate that the pagan world has long lain in error, and that Christians alone, through Christ and the prophets, have come to a true knowledge of God. Despite his title, the apologist's goal is often offensive; his concern is to show that divine truth has finally broken through the forces which have deceived humanity, and that this truth is found in the church and its prophets.[6]

Justin. This is particularly true of Justin, who lays much of the groundwork for later apologists. From the opening sections of his *First Apology,* Justin is concerned not merely with the defense of Christianity against its slanderers, but with the clash of two opposing views of knowledge and divine truth. To the most pious Caesar and his son Verissimus the philosopher, Justin says, "Reason (λόγος) directs those who are truly pious and philosophical to honour and love only what is true, declining to follow traditional opinions, if these be worthless."[7] Justin, on the grounds of logos, true piety, and true philosophy, asserts that the accomplishments of hellenistic culture are the products of ignorance and deception, and argues that humanity only succeeds in breaking daemonic deception when it receives the Logos revealed in the prophets and Christ. Inspiration and prophecy are at the heart of this offensive, because Justin argues that while the Christians are beneficiaries of revelation in the prophets and Christ, hellenistic culture has been for the most part inspired by daemons, who have successfully enslaved the human race.

Justin calls the daemons οἱ φαῦλοι δαίμονες (1 *apol.* 5) and accepts the current Jewish view of their origin. God gave the care of humanity to angels, and it is from these angels that the daemons come. Justin says, "But the angels transgressed this appointment, and were captivated by the love of women, and begat children who are those that are called daemons."[8] Subsequently, Justin says, they "subdued the

---

[6] Fiorenza has indicated the relationship between apologetic and missionary propaganda, and has shown the importance of miraculous powers and experiences in apologetic. Elisabeth Schüssler Fiorenza, "Miracles, Mission and Apologetic: An Introduction," in *Aspects of Religious Propaganda in Judaism and Early Christianity,* ed. Elisabeth Schüssler Fiorenza (Notre Dame: University of Notre Dame Press, 1976), p. 1-25.

[7] 1 *apol.* 2. See Robert M. Grant, *Greek Apologists of the Second Century* (Philadelphia: Westminster, 1988), p. 53.

[8] 2 *apol.* 5. This view is found in I Enoch. See Daniélou, *Jewish Christianity,* p. 187, and J.H. Waszink, ed., *Tertulliani De anima* (Amsterdam: J.M. Meulenhoff, 1947), p. 105, n. on 2.3 for references in the apologists.

human race to themselves" (2 *apol.* 5). Their goal has been to prevent
humanity from knowing God, and from rising above knowledge of
merely material things. According to Justin, the daemons act as jailers,
holding humanity as slaves and servants (1 *apol.* 14). He asserts,

> They who are called devils attempt nothing else than to seduce
> men from God who made them, and from Christ His first
> begotten; and those who are unable to raise themselves above
> earth they have riveted, and do now rivet to things earthly, and
> to the works of their own hands.[9]

The daemons have used every means at their disposal to carry out this
task, and here the issue of inspiration comes into play. Justin says,
"sometimes by appearances in dreams, and sometimes by magical
impositions, they subdue all who make no strong opposing effort for
their own salvation" (1 *apol.* 14). They have primarily carried out their
enslavement by inspiring the foundations of hellenistic religion and
culture. They taught humanity to sacrifice animals, since they stood in
need of offerings after their involvement in the passions (2 *apol.* 5).
They inspired the immoral literature and the stories of the gods on
which Greek culture was based. Justin argues that they accomplished
this in two ways. First, by apparitions and magic, the daemons
convinced the ignorant that they were gods. He says,

> since of old these evil demons, effecting apparitions of
> themselves, both defiled women and corrupted boys, and showed
> such fearful sights to men, that those who did not use their
> reason in judging of the actions that were done, were struck
> with terrors and being carried away by fear, and not knowing
> that these were demons, they called them gods.[10]

---

[9] 1 *apol.* 58.
[10] 1 *apol.* 5, ἐπεὶ τὸ παλαιὸν δαίμονες φαῦλοι, ἐπιφανείας
ποιησάμενοι, καὶ γυναῖκας ἐμοίχευσαν καὶ παῖδας διέφθειραν καὶ
φόβητρα ἀνθρώποις ἔδειξαν, ὡς καταπλαγῆναι τοὺς οἳ λόγῳ τὰς
γινομένας πράξεις οὐκ ἔκρινον, ἀλλὰ δέει συνηρπασμένοι καὶ μὴ
ἐπιστάμενοι δαίμονας εἶναι φαύλους, θεοὺς προσωνόμαζον.

Secondly, however, the daemons also directly inspired the poets. The myths were manufactured by the daemons to imitate the coming of the Logos in Christ, and the fraud was carried out by means of the poets. Justin says, "some, influenced by the demons . . . related beforehand, through the instrumentality of the poets, those circumstances as having really happened, which, having fictitiously devised, they narrated."[11] It was the daemons at work in the poets who produced the religious system of the Greeks.

Beyond the inspiration of Greek religion and culture, which was calculated to keep humanity in ignorance of divine truth, the daemons also made direct attacks upon Christianity. Where divine truth had penetrated the daemonic veil of deception, the demons caused those who had glimmers of the Logos, which Christians now have in full, to be persecuted. "It is by the influence of wicked demons," he says, "that earnest men, such as Socrates and the like, suffer persecution and are in bonds."[12] The demons have likewise instigated heresies to undermine the progress of Christianity. Simon, Meander, and Marcion were all "inspired by devils," and cause Christians to be slandered and God to be blasphemed (1 *apol*. 26). More directly, the daemons have used those whom they have successfully deceived to arrange the persecution of Christians themselves. Justin says, "the evil demons, who hate us, and who keep those who love pleasure subject to themselves, and serving them . . . incite them, as rulers actuated by evil spirits, to put us to death" (2 *apol*. 1). Justin urges the emperor to break this bondage and end the impious and irrational persecution of the Christians.

This brings us back to the passage quoted at the beginning of this chapter. The old man of the *Dialogue with Trypho* contrasts to the "false prophets, who are filled with a lying and unclean spirit," prophets "both righteous and beloved by God, who spoke by the Divine Spirit. . . . These alone both saw and announced the truth to men" (*Dial*. 7). Freedom from the deception of the daemons and their false inspiration is found only among the Christians, in their scriptures, and in Christ.

---

[11] *1 apol*. 23, φθάσαντές τινες, διὰ τοὺς προειρημένους κακοὺς δαίμονας διὰ τῶν ποιητῶν ὡς γενόμενα εἶπον ἃ μυθοποιήσαντες ἔφησαν.

[12] *2 apol*. 7. Socrates' crime, of course, consisted of casting out the poets and teaching men to reject daemons (2 *apol*. 10).

The proof of their conquest of the daemons is evident in their abstention from idolatry and their ability to cast the daemons out of those they possess (2 *apol.* 6). For Justin, only Christians, through the logos in the prophets and Christ, escape the debilitating effects of daemonic culture. He says, concerning baptism,

> Since at our birth we were born without our own knowledge or choice, by our parents coming together, and were brought up in bad habits and wicked training; in order that we may not remain the children of necessity and ignorance, but may become the children of choice and knowledge . . . there is pronounced over [the candidate] . . . the name of God the Father and Lord of the universe.[13]

For Justin, the issue between the Christian and Greek worlds is that of truth, power, and freedom against ignorance, deception, and enslavement. The debate over inspiration has been moved from the intramural struggle between claimants to the Christian tradition to the struggle between competing world views. In this context it is a practical and powerful polemical tool.

Tatian. Tatian presents the same type of argument concerning inspiration and spiritual conflict as Justin, with certain differences. It has long been noted that Tatian, while a student of Justin, is much more strident in his attack on Greek culture. Puech's observation concerning Justin and Tatian still stands: "Le second est aussi violent que le premier est doux."[14] Justin's view of the Greek world is a global one; the veil of ignorance cast by the daemons stands over human culture, with glimmers of truth breaking through, reflected in the high points of the Greek past. Tatian's view is more personal; the

---

[13]This is not to imply that Justin believes in determinism. He strongly affirms human freedom and the justice of God in assigning reward and punishment. However, freedom consists in moving from a bad to a good state, which is just what takes place in moving from enslavement of daemons to God. Christ, in his victory over the daemons, makes this possible.

[14]Aimé Puech, *Les apologistes Grecs du IIe siècle de notre ère* (Paris: Librairie Hachette, 1912), p. 148.

fallen daemons actively prevent souls from achieving their union with God. His scheme is the same as Justin's, however. Inspiration and prophecy stand at the center of his apologetic, because the conflict between Greek and Christian is the spiritual conflict of souls seeking God and the daemons who attempt to hold them in the earthly sphere.

According to Tatian, humanity was originally created with both soul and divine spirit, but lost the spirit because of disobedience (Tatian *Orat.* 7). Tatian uses the Platonic imagery of the soul's loss of wings to describe the fall, equating the spirit with the lost wings (*Orat.* 20.1). The soul is now alone in its union with the body, and in a state of spiritual ignorance. It retained a spark of the spirit, says Tatian, but this spark is insufficient to overcome its spiritual ignorance. As a result, the soul is alone and in darkness, and is attracted downward to matter and inferior beings. Its only hope lies in being reunited with the divine spirit. The spiritual life consists of the soul's attempts to re-ascend to union with the spirit and to knowledge of God (*Orat.* 15.1).

As a consequence of its loss of the spirit, the soul, in its attraction to matter, is vulnerable to the work of the daemons. According to Tatian, the daemons are those beings who followed the first-born of God's creatures, the devil, into rebellion (*Orat.* 7.2). Although they do not possess flesh, they are, he says, composed of matter.[15] By this, he means they are far down the scale of separation from God. All of creation is ordered into inferior and superior parts, and all of the world possesses, in varying degrees, the "material spirit." The daemons, because of their rebellion, are far down on this scale of matter, although they differ in degree within their ranks. Tatian says, "Nevertheless the demons too, as you call them who were compacted from matter and possess a spirit derived from it, became profligate and greedy, some of them turning to what is purer, others to what is inferior to matter and behaving like it."[16] Tatian calls them an army of "demonic apparitions" (τὰ φαντάσματα δαιμόνων, *Orat.* 7).

---

[15]They are composed of fire and air (*Orat.* 15.3).

[16]*Orat.* 15.3. Puech notes that this conception of a material spirit pervading creation is the Platonic world-soul, "mais qui est conçu plus spécialement à l'image du principe actif des stoiciens." Puech, *Les apologistes Grecs*, p. 57.

According to Tatian, "Men became the subject of the demons' apostasy" (*Orat.* 8). The soul, bereft of the spirit and drawn to matter, is susceptible to the "hostile devices" of the daemons who hinder its ascent. The daemons, by means of appearances, magic, and divination, attack both the body and the mind to keep the soul from learning the truth (*Orat.* 17-19). They are also the administrators of fate, according to Tatian, and, by ordering the stars, introduced mythology and astrology. Tatian says, "For they showed men a chart of the constellations, and like dice-players they introduced the factor of fate -- a very unjust one -- which brought both judge and prisoner to where they are now" (*Orat.* 8.1). Since the fall, they have been actively waging war against human souls, to prevent the successful reunion of the soul with the divine spirit. Tatian says,

> For the demons in their own malignity rage against men, and by various false machinations pervert their thoughts when they incline downwards, in order that they may not have the power to rise aloft for the heavenly journey.[17]

The result is a spiritual conflict in which only those who have been enlightened by true prophecy and association with the spirit of God prevail. Those souls who succeed in union with God overcome the "false machination of the demons." Tatian says of the soul, "if it lives alone it inclines down towards matter and dies with the flesh, but if it gains union with the divine spirit it is not unaided, but mounts to the realms above where the spirit leads it" (*Orat.* 13.1). He argues that some have achieved this union by obedience, and proclaim the truth about God to the rest who are kept in ignorance by the daemons: "God's spirit is not given to all, but dwelling among some who behaved justly and being intimately connected with the soul it revealed by predictions to the other souls what had been hidden" (*Orat.* 13.3). These are the prophets, and only by listening to them, and inclining one's soul upward, can one escape the captivity of the daemons. Those who are so enlightened are then able to perceive the spiritual bodies of the daemons (*Orat.* 15.4) and escape the restraining force of fate. "We are

---

[17]*Orat.* 16.1.

above fate," says Tatian, "and instead of planetary demons we have come to know one lord who does not err; we are not led by fate and have rejected its lawgivers" (*Orat.* 9.2). The Christians, as those united to the spirit, thus escape the pull of material things which keeps the Greeks captive in astrology, magic, and divination, and, because of the prophets, have a knowledge which "is above worldly comprehension" (*Orat.* 12.4).

For Tatian, as for Justin, inspiration and prophecy play a crucial role in apologetic. On the one hand, the false inspiration of the daemons captures humanity by means of such manifestations as apparitions, magic, divination, and astrology. On the other hand, the prophets, united with the spirit of God, rescue the soul from this captivity with the proclamation of the truth, and make it possible for the soul to ascend to reunion with the divine spirit. Tatian's apologetic treatment thus emphasizes concepts of personal significance, such as spiritual power and freedom, as well as the conflict of worldviews.

Tertullian.   Tertullian's apologetic presents the same type of argument as that evident in Justin and Tatian.[18] While Tertullian bases his defense of the Scriptures on the proofs of antiquity and fulfillment (Tertullian *Apol.* 19.1), he argues that error and ignorance of divine truth are due to the false inspiration of Greek culture by the daemons. He says,

> Everything against the Truth is built up from the Truth, and it is the spirits of error that produce this rivalry. It is they who have produced these falsifications of wholesome doctrine; they who have launched the fables, which by their resemblance weaken the credibility of Truth or rather capture belief for themselves.[19]

Tertullian, like the other apologists, feels that the goal of the daemons is to prevent the enlightenment and salvation of humanity. According to Tertullian, "Their work is the ruin of man" (*Apol.* 22.4).

---

[18]Tertullian knew the work of Justin. So Timothy Barnes, *Tertullian: A Historical and Literary Study* (Oxford: Clarendon Press, 1971), p. 108.

[19]*Apol.* 47.11.

They attack the body with sicknesses and injuries, but also attack the mind. Their inspiration (*adspiratio*) corrupts the mind and causes frenzy, insanity, lust and error, while "of all delusions that is the greatest which they use to recommend those gods to the captive and outwitted minds of men" (*Apol.* 22.6). They have successfully enslaved Greek culture and, Tertullian says, the daemonic spirit "battles against us with your hearts for his base" (*Apol.* 27.4).

Tertullian's well-known vituperations against Greek culture are in part based on his view of the daemonic inspiration of hellenistic life. According to Tertullian, the non-Christian soul begins its association with daemons at its inception. To take part in almost any civic or social function is to be involved with daemons, and to be subject to their influence. This begins at birth, when, as a result of natal ceremonies, the soul acquires an evil familiar spirit. Tertullian rejects the Platonic division of the soul into a higher, rational part and a lower, irrational part, and argues that at birth the rational soul exists alone, without any evil (or divine) influence. Tertullian says, "It is the rational element which we must believe to be its natural condition. ... The irrational element, however, we must understand to have accrued later, as having proceeded from the instigation of the serpent" (Tertullian *De an.* 16). The evil influence on the soul is added when the soul acquires a *daemon paredros*, a familiar daemon which accompanies it throughout life and keeps it in ignorance and wickedness. According to Tertullian,

> All these endowments of the soul which are bestowed on it at birth are still obscured and depraved by the malignant being. ... For to what individual of the human race will not the evil spirit cleave, ready to entrap their souls from the portal of their birth, at which he is invited to be present in all those superstitious processes which accompany childbearing?[20]

---

[20]*De an.* 39. See Waszink, *De anima*, p. 442-447 for a discussion of these ceremonies. Waszink asserts that Tertullian is not speaking of the indwelling of an evil daemon at birth, but only the devil's efforts to capture the soul (p. 447). However, Tertullian's *adhaerebit* indicates a strong connection between the daemon and the soul: Cui enim hominum non adhaerebit spiritus nequam ab ipsa etiam

Christians alone are free from this daemonic inspiration. Tertullian argues that the Christians, who have power to cast out the daemons, are the only mitigating influence in human society, and if they ever wish revenge for the persecutions, need only stop casting out daemons to find sufficient satisfaction (*Apol.* 27.9). Christian spiritual power and freedom in the face of the false inspiration of the daemons is emphasized by Tertullian in this way:

> Bring forward some or other of those persons who are supposed to be god-possessed, who by sniffing at altars inhale a divine power in the smell, who cure themselves by belching, who declaim panting. ... Let any Christian you please bid him speak and the spirit in the man will own himself a demon.[21]

The argument over inspiration thus consists of a consideration of the evil influences of the daemons, their power, and the freedom and power to be found in Christian prophecy and scriptures. For Tertullian, as for the other apologists, inspiration and prophecy are central to the apologetic task.

Athenagoras. Inspiration and prophecy are equally important in the apologetic of Athenagoras. Athenagoras uses contemporary understandings of prophecy and divination to argue, in much the same way as the other apologists, that pagan religion is the result of false inspiration, that is, that it derives from the movements of fallen angels and wicked daemons.

As we indicated in the previous chapter, prophecy in the ancient world was often held to derive from a stirring, excitement, or movement of the prophetic faculty of the soul. Athenagoras uses this language of movement to describe what takes place in prophecy, and especially in the deceptive activities of the daemons. According to Athenagoras, the soul is properly moved by reason (logos) and its affinity to God. Like Justin, Athenagoras attributes any truth attained by the poets and philosophers to this affinity with God and its moving of the soul, and

---

ianua nativitatis animas aucupabundus, vel qua invitatus tota illa puerperii superstitione?

[21]*Apol.* 23.4.

he describes it in prophetic language. He says, "For poets and philosophers have gone at this and other matters by guesswork, each of them moved by his own soul through some affinity with the breath of God (κινηθέντες μὲν κατὰ συμπάθειαν τῆς παρὰ τοῦ θεοῦ πνοῆς)."[22] The prophets, however, were moved by the Holy Spirit (κινήσαντος αὐτοὺς τοῦ θείου πνεύματος), and it is in this sense that Athenagoras uses the common image of the prophet as the flute, played by the divine flautist.[23]

The soul, however, is susceptible to other movements. Because of human association with matter, the soul is particularly vulnerable to the moving of the daemons, who have themselves fallen into lust for matter.[24] According to Athenagoras, the daemons have so inspired humanity as to produce the errors of Greek philosophy and religion. He says, concerning the mistaken opinions of the philosophers,

> But since the demonic impulses and activities of the hostile spirit bring these wild attacks -- indeed we see them move men from within and from without, one man one way and another man another, some individually and some as nations, one at a time and all together, because of our kinship with matter and our affinity with the divine.[25]

This movement is most evident in the stimulation of idolatry, and Athenagoras describes this in language similar to hellenistic discussions of untrustworthy dreams and divination.[26] According to Athenagoras, the soul, when it is weak and ignorant, is susceptible to the attacks of

---

[22]Athenagoras *Leg.* 7.2.

[23]*Leg.* 9.1, See Philo *Rer. div. her.* 1.510; Johannes Geffcken, *Zwei griechische Apologeten*, p. 180; and Paul Lejay, "Le plectre, la langue et l'Esprit," *Bulletin d'ancienne littérature et d'archeologie chrétiennes* 2 (1912):43-45.

[24]Athenagoras divides evil spirits into two groups, the fallen angels, and the daemons who are their offspring. They both, he says, produce movements, the daemons "movements which are akin to the nature they have received," and the fallen angels "movements which are akin to the lusts with which they were possessed." *Leg.* 25.1.

[25]*Leg.* 25.3

[26]See Plutarch *De def. or.* 414 E, 432 D, and Geffcken, *Apologeten*, p. 180, n. 1.

the daemons. They, in an effort to produce a belief in idols, invade the soul and produce φαντασίαι which deceive it into honoring them through idols. He says, "it is their business to delude men, [they] take hold of these deceitful movements in the soul of the many, and by invading their thoughts flood them with illusory images which seem to come from the idols and statues."[27]

Thus, inspiration provides significant ammunition in the apologetic arsenal of Athenagoras. Hellenistic, non-Christian culture, because of the inspiring movements of the daemons, is irrational and entrenched in the material and daemonic. Christianity, on the other hand, because of the influence of the divine affinity of the soul, and the movement of the prophets by the Holy Spirit, is rational, heavenly, and divine.

Other Apologists. These sorts of arguments are echoed in the other apologists as well. Theophilus argues that the poets were inspired by daemons, and asserts that Homer and Hesiod spoke "from a deceptive fancy, and not with a pure but an erring spirit" (Theophilus *Auto.* 2.7). Clement says of the guardian daemons of contemporary thought, "being intent upon your destruction, they beset human life after the manner of flatterers" (Clement *Prot.* 1). The summary statement of the *Exhortation to the Greeks* of pseudo-Justin, perhaps contemporary with Origen, sums up the central role which debate over inspiration played in the apologetic conflict:

> From every point of view, therefore, it must be seen that in no other way than only from the prophets who teach us by divine inspiration, is it at all possible to learn anything concerning God and the true religion.[28]

This type of argument is also evident in the more popular polemic between groups claiming divine truth and power. As we have indicated, much of the debate over prophecy in the second century centered around extraordinary figures who claim the status of inspired sage and divine

---

[27]*Leg.* 27.2, αἱ οὖν ἄλογοι αὗται καὶ ἰνδαλματώδεις τῆς ψυχῆς κινήσεις εἰδωλομανεῖς ἀποτίκτουσι φαντασίας.

[28]*Coh. Gr.* 38.

man. The sort of polemic evident in the works of Lucian and
Philostratus may also be found in the Christian world, and the
'philosophical' debate of the apologists is given practical form in such
conflicts as that of Irenaeus against certain figures, and that evident in
the Clementine literature.

POLEMIC

Irenaeus. Irenaeus, while not engaged directly in apologetic, is
certainly involved in polemic with Gnostic and other groups who claim
to possess divine knowledge and power. Much of this polemic centers
around the teachers and leaders who claim to possess such knowledge
and power, particularly such figures as Marcus, whose claims include
the ability to prophesy and work wonders. Features of prophecy which
are important to the Christian community are thus evident in the
attacks which Irenaeus makes on Marcus and others like him. In
dealing with the errors of such figures, Irenaeus is particularly concerned
with the use of magic, dependence upon a familiar spirit, and
inspiration by the false or empty spirit.

According to Irenaeus, Marcus presents himself as one descended from
above, full of divine power and secret knowledge. One of his foremost
activities is prophecy; he claims to be able to prophesy himself, and to
be able to give this power to others. Irenaeus attacks this claim to
divine knowledge in several ways. He first of all argues that Marcus,
rather than possessing divine power, is actually a magician, who brings
off his wonders by magic. "He is," says Irenaeus, "a perfect adept at
magical impostures" (Irenaeus *Haer.* 1.13.1), and Irenaeus cites Marcus'
well-known trick with the cups as a means used to deceive his audience.
Irenaeus also charges that Marcus uses potions and love-philters to
capture his women, who, when liberated by the church, tell of their
magically induced passion (*Haer.* 1.13.5). In accordance with the charge
of magic, Irenaeus also asserts that Marcus accomplishes his wonders
and prophecy by means of the magician's familiar spirit, the *daemon
paredros.* He says, "It seems probable enough that this man possesses a
demon as his familiar spirit, by means of whom he seems able to

prophesy" (*Haer*. 1.13.3). In much the same manner as the critics of Apollonius, Irenaeus, in dealing with the divine claims of Marcus, presents him as a γόης rather than a θείος ἀνήρ.[29]

More importantly, however, Irenaeus attacks the spirit at work in Marcus and his female followers. Reiling has shown the dependence of Irenaeus on Hermas in this instance, and Irenaeus' concerns are similar to those of the *Shepherd* ; that is, to show that the false prophet is inspired by a weak, earthly daemon, rather than by the powerful spirit of God.[30] Irenaeus describes the means by which Marcus makes his female disciples prophesy:

> She then, vainly puffed up and elated by these words, and greatly excited in soul by the expectation that it is herself who is to prophesy, her heart beating violently, reaches the requisite pitch of audacity, and idly as well as impudently utters some nonsense as it happens to occur to her, such as might be expected from one heated by an empty spirit.[31]

Her soul, artificially excited and stirred, is vulnerable to the empty spirit, who causes her to prophesy, and thus deludes her. Like Hermas, Irenaeus says that those not full of faith will be filled by such empty spirits.[32] These spirits are "earthly and weak, audacious and impudent, sent forth by Satan for the seduction and perdition of those who do not hold fast that well-compacted faith" (*Haer*. 1.13.4). Marcus and his cohorts are consorting with earthly daemons, rather than the Holy Spirit, and this involves them in the entire range of magical deception, from such false wonders as the cup trick to frenzy and susceptibility to apparitions and phantasms.

This sort of polemic is standard issue in Irenaeus' attacks on false prophets and teachers. Like the Marcosians, the followers of Simon practice magic, exorcisms, and incantations. According to Irenaeus, "Love-potions too, and charms, as well as those beings who are called

---

[29]Reiling shows that like Hermas, Irenaeus, in his criticism of Marcus, is aiming at hellenistic prophetic practices. Reiling, *Hermas*, p. 95.

[30]Ibid., p. 85.

[31]*Haer*. 1.13.1.

[32] *Haer*. 1.16.3. He quotes Matt. 12:43, about the seven wicked spirits.

Paredri (familiars) and Oneiropompi (dream-senders), and whatever other
curious arts can be had recourse to, are eagerly pressed into their service
(*Haer*. 1.23)." The Carpocratians also use familiar spirits and dream-
senders (*Haer*. 1.25), and such groups, says Irenaeus, "are altogether full
of deceit of every kind, apostate inspiration, demoniacal working, and
the phantasms of idolatry."[33]
It is clear, then, that in polemic dealing with claimants to divine
power and truth, prophecy and inspiration play a large part. Irenaeus'
efforts are to demonstrate that with such alleged divine men as Marcus,
their wonders and prophecy are in reality the work of earthly demons,
and they are rather to be considered γόητες. As such, they are
involved in magic, dependent on familiar spirits and other daemons, and
are associated with deceiving wonders such as phantasms and
apparitions. In this type of polemic, as in that of the apologists, the
issue is one of power and freedom from delusion.

The Clementine Literature. The Clementine literature provides a
unique, although sometimes enigmatic, opportunity to examine
polemic concerning prophecy, inspiration, the figure of the wonder-
worker, and the work of the daemons. In much the same way as
hellenistic polemic found in such romantic literature as Philostratus'
Life of Apollonius, the Clementine *Homilies* and *Recognitions* set
forth an amalgam of debate and discussion over prophecy and
inspiration within the setting of an ancient novel. We are presented
with the attacks and counterattacks of Simon Magus and the apostle
Peter, while being entertained by the story of Clement's serendipitous
'recognition' of his long lost brothers, mother and father. While the
extant forms of the *Homilies* and *Recognitions* are later in date than
the period which we have been reviewing, it is probable that their
foundational material goes back at least to the end of our period,[34] and

---

[33] *Haer*. 2.31.2. This is standard Christian polemic. Justin accuses the pagans
of using ὀνειροπομποὶ καὶ πάρεδροι (1 *apol*. 18), and Tertullian speaks of
magicians, somnia immittunt habentes semel invitatorum angelorum et daemonum
adsistentem sibi potestatem (*Apol*. 23.1).

[34] For a discussion of the scholarly assessment of the Clementine literature see
F. Stanley Jones, "The Pseudo-Clementines: A History of Research," *Second
Century* 2 (1982):1-33, 63-96. For positive and negative responses to the

they include arguments evident in the apologists and other early Christian literature.[35] In the debates between Simon Magus and Peter, they provide a collection of the arguments concerning prophecy and inspiration used in the Christian tradition. It is clear in this literature that prophecy is a central concern. Christ is identified primarily as the True Prophet,[36] and most of the discussion is directed towards questions of true and false prophecy and inspiration, and the means of finding and following the true prophet. The homilist says,

> On this account the whole business of religion needed a true prophet, that he might tell us things that are, as they are, and how we must believe concerning all things. So that it is first necessary to test the prophet by every prophetic sign, and having ascertained that he is true, thereafter to believe him in everything.[37]

The direction of this polemic is evident in the picture given of Simon, the preaching of Peter on daemons and prophecy, and the teachings given on true revelation and prophecy.

Although Simon is given a chance to defend himself in the *Homilies* and *Recognitions*, the text is decidedly hostile to him. He is presented as a wandering wonder-worker or γόης who has prophetic and supernatural powers, and uses them to proclaim his divinity and attract and deceive a following. Like any good sorcerer, he made the

---

question of whether Origen knew some form of the Clementines, see Renè Cadiou, "Origène et les 'reconnaissances clémentines'," *Recherches de science religieuse* 20 (1932):517; and Georg Strecker, *Das Judenchristentum in den Pseudoklementinen* (Berlin: Akademie Verlag, 1981), pp. 263-264.

[35]For example, *Clem. Rec.* 5.30, gives the pagan argument from custom, while 5.27 and 5.29 echo pagan arguments on polytheism and providence given by Celsus. Compare Origen *Cels.* 8.2, and 4.99.

[36]The title of True Prophet represents almost the full scope of Christological speculation, and on this basis the Clementine literature is usually associated with a Jewish-Christian sect such as the Ebionites or Elchasites. See J. Irmscher, "The Pseudo-Clementines," in Edgar Hennecke, *New Testament Apocrypha*, ed. Wilhelm Schneelmelcher, trans. R. McL. Wilson, vol. 2 (Philadelphia: Westminster, 1965), pp. 533-534.

[37]*Hom. Clem.* 1.19.

obligatory trip to Egypt to study magic,[38] and now, says the homilist, "wishes to be accounted a certain supreme power, greater even than the God who created the world."[39] His wonders are achieved by the manipulation of phantasms and hallucinations (φαντάσματα καὶ ἰνδάλματα), and "when he walks abroad, statues move, and many shadows go before him which, he says, are souls of the dead" (*Hom. Clem.* 4.4).

His primary means of magic and prophecy, however, is the use of a familiar, the soul of a dead boy. Simon boasts of how he separated the soul from the body of a boy "unsullied and violently slain,"[40] reformed the body out of air, painted a picture of the reconstituted body and hung it over his bed, and then redissolved the body. "By it," he says, "all is done that I command" (*Rec. Clem.* 2.13). Simon's prophecy is not the divine foreknowledge that he makes it out to be; rather the text wishes to indicate that he is involved in the black art, and has intercourse with phantoms and dead souls. Beyond that, Peter asserts that Simon himself is deluded about the nature of the soul of the boy; it is not a soul at all, but a daemon which deceives him into thinking he sees the substance of the soul.[41]

Simon is also represented as possessing suspect views of the ways of attaining knowledge of God and revelation. He allegedly depends upon the appearance of images, which can be found in imagination, visions, or dreams. With respect to imagination, Simon uses language similar to the eye of the soul terminology, and urges Peter, if he wishes to see divine truth, to reach out with his mind: "In this way now reach forth

---

[38]*Hom. Clem.* 2.22, cf. Origen *Cels.* 1.68.

[39]*Hom. Clem.* 2.22, *Rec. Clem.* 2.7. Justin (1 *apol.* 26), Irenaeus (*Haer.* 1.23), and Tertullian (*De an.* 34), record this claim.

[40]*Clem. Rec.* 2.13. Tertullian accuses the magicians of killing children to obtain oracles (*Apol.* 23.1), while Apuleius notes that the souls of young boys are particularly suited for divination, which can be achieved by "the allurement of music or the soothing influence of sweet smells" (*Apol.* 43). Philostratus (*VA* 3.48) says that a demon possessing a boy was the soul of a man slain in war, a βιαιοθάνατος; see Jacques Puiggali, "La démonologie de Philostrate," *Revue des sciences philosophique et theologique* 67 (1983):123.

[41]To strengthen this point, the homilist has Simon himself confess that the soul of the boy is actually a daemon (*Hom. Clem.* 2.30).

your sense into heaven, yea above the heaven, and behold that there must be some place beyond the world" (*Rec. Clem.* 2.61). Peter responds, however, that such imagination is not to be trusted, since what is perceived is only a φαντασία (*Rec. Clem.* 2.65). Andrew, who rebukes Peter for succumbing to this kind of reverie, says,

> For those who are beginning to be possessed with a demon, or to be disturbed in their minds, begin in this way. They are first carried away by fancies to some pleasant and delightful things, then they are poured out in vain and fond motions towards things which have not existence. Now this happens from a certain disease of mind, by reason of which they see not the things which are, but long to bring to their sight those which are not.[42]

Such recourse to imagination results in the production of multiple images, and ultimately, frenzy. Simon also argues that true knowledge of God comes from apparitions and visions, rather than through what one has 'seen and heard', as the apostles claim.[43] The mind cannot implicitly trust information received through the senses, but visions and apparitions can be accepted at face value because they are sent from God. He says, "visions and dreams, being God-sent, do not speak falsely in regard to those matters which they wish to tell" (*Hom. Clem.* 17.15). This, however, is only another indication of Simon's deception by daemons. Peter replies that, while all God-sent dreams indeed do tell the truth, not all visions and dreams are God-sent. Visions, dreams, and apparitions are seen equally by the impious, particularly by those who take part in idolatry, and they are more likely to be the work of deceptive daemons. He says,

> But he who trusts to apparition or vision and dream is insecure. For he does not know to whom he is trusting. For it is

---

[42]*Rec. Clem.* 2.64.

[43]*Hom. Clem.* 17.13. This discussion is placed in the context of the Stoic/Academic debate over the reliance of the sense impression as a criterion of truth. See Robert J. Hauck, "'They Saw What They Said They Saw': Sense

> possible that either he may be an evil demon or a deceptive
> spirit, pretending in his speeches to be what he is not.[44]

Only the appropriately accredited prophet can be fully trusted, and such
a prophet does not depend on visions and apparitions (*Hom. Clem.*
17.14).

It is clear from this portrayal of Simon that one of the major
concerns of the debate over prophecy in this type of polemic is that of
magic and the daemonic.   Simon claims to have great powers of
prophecy and miracle. He himself, however, confides that his power
comes through the agency of the souls of the dead, and his prophecy
from visions and apparitions. The Clementine author then goes on to
show that this is a shaky foundation for divine knowledge; Simon, in
both areas, is in fact deluded by daemons. The conflict over prophecy
once again focuses on the person of the prophet, and his ability to
escape the deceptive powers of the daemons.

Peter carries out his part in the debate by preaching about the
daemons and their deceptive influence on humanity. He accepts the
traditional view that the daemons are descended from the giants, and
affirms that the lower angels exert a deceptive power as well (*Hom.
Clem.* 8.12, 14, 18). The daemons are hostile to people, and desire to
keep them bound in the material world so that the daemons can satisfy
their passions through human beings (*Rec. Clem.* 2.72, 4.16).
According to Peter, however, the daemons only influence those who
provide them an opportunity, and have been given a law which prevents
them from invading the souls of those who avoid them (*Hom. Clem.*
8.19). The majority of the human race, however, has allowed an
opening to the daemons through wickedness, immoderation, and
idolatry. Taking part in pagan religious festivals makes one a "table-
companion" of daemons (*Hom. Clem.* 8.20), and Peter says, "everyone
who has at any time worshipped idols, and has adored those whom the
pagans call gods, or has eaten of things sacrificed to them, is not
without an unclean spirit; for he has become a guest of demons, and has

---

Knowledge in Early Christian Polemic," *Harvard Theological Review* 81
(1988):239-249.

[44]*Hom. Clem.* 17.14.

been partaker with that demon of which he has formed the image in his mind, either through fear or love" (*Rec. Clem.* 2.71). Faith drives out the daemons, but the Clementine author, like Hermas, argues that complete purity is required in order to be entirely free from them; that part of the soul which is not occupied by faith and obedience is inhabited by daemons (*Rec. Clem.* 4.18).

It is daemonic activity which is most important in the discussion of prophecy. As we have seen, Peter argues that Simon has been deceived by daemons, and that all those who participate in idolatry, or seek divine truth through visions and dreams, are subject to their hostile influences. This deceptive influence takes many forms. Peter tells us that it was the fallen angels who originally taught magic to the human race (*Hom. Clem.* 8.14). More importantly, they also brought idolatry, and much of their deception is associated with the rites and festivals of the idols. In conjunction with the idols, they provide remedies and oracles to gain worship and obedience. They also appear in dreams and visions to maintain belief in the idols. They are able to be present in the souls of their believers, and appear as gods to those whom they hold captive.[45] When idol-worshippers meet daemons at the idols, the daemons cause all sorts of false inspirations and impulses. Peter says,

> And thus, of those who are present, some are filled with inspirations, and some with strange friends, and some betake themselves to lasciviousness, and some to theft and murder. For the exhalation of blood, and the libation of wine satisfies even these unclean spirits, which lurk within you and cause you to take pleasure in the things that are transacted there, and in dreams surround you with false phantasies, and punish you with myriads of diseases.[46]

Beyond inspiring idolatry, the daemons are able to suggest thoughts and desires within the minds of those who give them opportunity. Peter says they live within the bodies of human beings and incline "the motions of their souls to those things which they themselves desire"

---

[45]*Hom. Clem.* 9.16. According to Peter, the fact that gods never appear to the Jews is proof that these apparitions are really daemons.

[46]*Hom. Clem.* 11.15.

(*Rec. Clem.* 2.72). He speaks of the "evil-working suggestion of the deceiving serpent that is in you, which seduces you by the promise of better reason, creeping from your brain to your spinal marrow, and setting great value upon deceiving you" (*Hom. Clem.* 10.10). Those thus deceived are not able to perceive these inspirations of the daemons, and think that they come from their own souls (*Hom. Clem.* 9.12, 14). These inspirations are generally to enable the daemons to satisfy their desires, but an equal goal, according to Peter, is that humanity may neglect salvation.

In the face of this false prophecy of the daemons, Peter's side of the polemic argues for a picture of true revelation. Peter asserts that true prophecy has nothing to do with familiar spirits, daemons, dreams or visions. Rather, the true prophet has prophetic knowledge at all times, not just while in a trance, and receives intuitive knowledge rather than visions. Peter says,

> But if we should hold, as many do, that even the true Prophet, not always, but sometimes, when He has the Spirit, and through it, foreknows, but when He has it not is ignorant, -- if we should suppose thus, we should deceive ourselves and mislead others. For such a matter belongs to those who are madly inspired by the spirit of disorder.[47]

Rather than relying upon the aid of a helping spirit to attain knowledge, the true prophet gains knowledge of God which does not leave him. This occurs because the prophet is not simply given a message to hand on, but the knowledge of God, entrenched in the soul, is made available to him. He stands as the example of the pious and wise man, the sage who has grown in ability to see divine truth. The Clementine author claims the authority of Peter for this point of view:

---

[47]*Hom. Clem.* 3.13.

It came into my [Peter's] heart to say, . . . 'Thou art the Son of the living God.' But He . . . pointed out to me that it was the Father who had revealed it to me; and from this time I learned that revelation is knowledge gained without instruction, and without apparition and dreams. . . . For in the soul which has been placed in us by God, there is all the truth; but it is covered and revealed by the hand of God who works so far as each one through his knowledge deserves.[48]

The conflict is thus between the intuitive knowledge of one whose soul knows God, and the visions, apparitions, and phantasms of the false prophet.

The Clementine literature, like the anti-Gnostic polemic of Irenaeus, provides an enlightening background for Christian debates about prophecy. Like that of the apologists, this literature emphasizes the spiritual conflict which takes place in prophecy. Here, however, centered around the figure of a wonder worker or divine man, the conflict is much more personal. The question is whether a given prophet actually has divine knowledge. The issues involved are the use of familiar spirits, dependence upon daemons, and deception by apparitions and visions. The true prophet is one who escapes such entanglements, and by purity of soul attains knowledge of God.

CONCLUSION

The Christian tradition thus displays a long and rich discussion of true and false prophecy, particularly in the context of apologetic. Significant features of the Christian background for the debate of the *Against Celsus* include discussions of the false inspiration of daemons, involvement in magic and dependence upon familiar spirits, and reliance upon apparitions, visions, and phantasms for prophetic knowledge.

This background also indicates the significance of inspiration as an apologetic tool. Christian apologetic, consisting of both defense and

---

[48]*Hom. Clem.* 17.18.

propaganda, presents the conflict of pagan and Christian as a cosmic one, carried out in the spiritual realm, where soul struggles with daemon in a battle for spiritual freedom and truth. At issue are two opposing ways of viewing the world and the achievements of culture and religion. In the debates over prophecy, however, this issue is brought down to the practical and immediate realm of personal freedom and power. The Christian world argued that Greek culture, with all its accomplishments, was actually under the false inspiration of the wicked daemons, while only the Christians, enlightened by prophets who truly knew divine truth, were able to see the enslaving work of those daemons. For the Christians, the choice was between slavery and ignorance in a culture deluded by daemons, and the freedom and knowledge brought by the ancient prophets and the Logos.

Chapter 4

"Phantoms and Terrors:"

Celsus on Christian Prophecy

> If you shut your eyes to the world of sense
> and look up with the mind, if you turn away
> from the flesh and raise the eyes of the soul,
> only so will you see God. And if you look
> for someone to lead you along this path, you
> must flee from the deceivers and sorcerers
> who court phantoms. *Cels.* 7.36.

Celsus, roughly contemporary with Irenaeus, attacks Christianity
with the same combination of observer's acumen and outsider's
vehemence that Irenaeus uses with the Gnostics. His critique of
Christian prophetic knowledge follows many of the themes which we
have already seen, and possesses a coherent scheme for determining true
prophecy and divine knowledge. The "ancient and inspired" founders of
the Greek tradition were θεῖοι, the Christian founders were φαῦλοι;
and Celsus has a consistent argument, based on his understanding of
inspiration, the knowledge of God, and the daemons, to prove it.

THE QUESTION

The philosophy of the second century is often considered to represent
a decline from the golden days of the great founders, usually because of
the hardening of school lines, its dependence upon tradition, and its

corruption of the pure rationalism which had characterized the great age of Greece. The turning of thinkers to religious questions, and their apparent attraction to mysticism, ecstaticism, and the supernatural, seen in the extreme in Gnosticism, are all viewed as symptoms of the stagnation and decadence of imperial thought.

The place of Celsus on this slippery slope of decline into superstition is one of some controversy. Some see him as the voice of rationalism, crying out against the tide of fideism swelling within Christianity.[1] Others have noted that side of Celsus' thought that supports divination, astrology, incubation, magic, idolatry, and the mystery cults.[2] Well aware, however, of his philosophical arguments against the Christians, his dislike of their fideism, and his distaste for the vulgarity of their myth and rites, such scholars have usually argued that there is an unresolved tension in Celsus' thought between his allegiance to popular cult and practice, and his intellectual attack on the Christians.

Anna Miura-Stange represents the latter approach in her characterization of Celsus' polemic. According to Miura-Stange, Celsus must hide the weakness and the contradictory nature of his argument, "die Schwäche, insofern er, der die Vernunft einzig entscheiden lassen will, doch selbst den pietätsvollen Glauben und die Autorität des Alters in Anspruch nimmt -- das Widerspruchsvolle, insofern er, der den fremden Mythus bekämpft, doch, selbst die eigene mythische Religionsstufe verteidigt."[3] Miura-Stange notes Celsus' aristocratic dislike for the magic loved by the "rabble," but feels that Celsus' own attraction to superstition is manifested by a love for astrology and ornithomancy.[4]

---

[1]For example, Louis Rougier characterizes the apologetic debate between the Christians and Celsus as a battle between religion and science, faith and reason, revelation and rationality. *Celse contre les Chrétiens*, p. 46.

[2]Henri Crouzel says, "rien n'est plus faux que de le considérer comme le 'Voltaire du second siècle.' " Henri Crouzel, "Conviction intérieure et aspects extérieurs de la religion chez Celse et Origène," *Bulletin de littérature ecclésiastique* 77 (1976):83.

[3]Miura-Stange, *Celsus und Origenes*, p. 16.

[4]Ibid., p. 105, "Noch tiefer in den Aberglauben hinein führen seine überraschenden Aussagen über weissagende Vögel usw."

Pierre de Labriolle echoes this approach in his discussion of the "incertitudes" of Celsus. Labriolle says, "C'est dans une atmosphère d'intime contradiction qu'elle opère et qu'elle vit."[5] According to Labriolle, Celsus appears to be a rationalizing skeptic, but there lives in the heart of his thought an attachment to the popular cult. Labriolle says, "Si Celse est, au fond, detáché des croyances populaires, il a gardé cependant une sorte de religiosité qui se trahit par accès et rejoint en certains cas les superstitions courante."[6]

Unlike the previously mentioned scholars, Carl Andresen both affirms the incongruity in Celsus' thought, and attempts to resolve it. Taking issue with Miura-Stange's complacency with the *Widerspruchsvolle* of Celsus' system, Andresen seeks a theme which will unify the fragments of Celsus which deal with wonders and popular piety. Andresen finds this theme in Celsus' concept of history. He finds contradictions in Celsus' thought in three areas, the treatment of wonders, of myth, and of the mystery religions. In all these areas, the ambiguous character of Celsus' statements can be explained by his concern for the historical character of the ancient logos. The wonders which Celsus accepts are not simply stories in his eyes, but true occurrences of wonder-working skill which are confirmed through history, in both past and present.[7] The crucial criterion is reputation, or authority (*Ansehen*). The same is true in the area of myth. In spite of his critical approach, Celsus has eminent regard for the traditional, historical character of the ancient myths, which allows him to use them as a source for the logos.[8] The mystery religions, which are sometimes the object of his sarcasm, also bear the weight of tradition and history. Since they represent the traditions of ancient peoples such as the Egyptians, they equally convey the historical, universal wisdom. For Celsus, the key to distinguishing between the true mysteries and the false, such as Christianity, is historical attestation. According to

---

[5]Labriolle, *La réaction païenne*, p. 131.

[6]Ibid., p. 132.

[7]"Was Kelsos z. B. in frr. III, 22-33 vorträgt, sind für ihn keine "Historien" im Sinne von Legenden, wie Origenes sie bezeichnet, sondern wirkliches Geschehen wundersamer Art, das durch die Geschichte in Vergangenheit und Gegenwart bestätigt wird." Andresen, *Logos und Nomos*, p. 50.

[8]Ibid., p. 55.

Andresen, Celsus here parts company from his fellow Platonists in making truth depend upon empirical historical fact, rather than upon theoretical knowledge.[9]

With regard to the issues of piety and the knowledge of God, Andresen also sees an inner contradiction which is resolved by the concept of history. According to Andresen, a distinction is made by Celsus between official and personal piety, as well as between immediate knowledge of God and that mediated by the daemons. Public piety uses the gods of the stars and the planets as mediators of divine revelation who convey to all men the knowledge of God. Private piety is characterized by immediate knowledge of God acquired by Platonic methods of abstraction, negation, and synthesis. This distinction in the matter of piety is echoed in the area of knowledge of God. There is a knowledge of God mediated by the daemons, and a knowledge which is acquired directly, without mediation. In both these areas, according to Andresen, there is a strained opposition in Celsus' thought.[10]

Andresen argues that the connecting link between these two forms of God-knowledge is the concept of history. Each nation has its piety, which is administered by its own daemons. The logos is dispensed in the cult of these ancient inspired nations, and so the principle of historical continuity provides the connection between national piety, administered by the daemons, and personal knowledge of God. Andresen thus argues that Celsus is working with an historically constructed argument, rather than with a religious-philosophical one.[11]

The issue of prophecy, inspiration, and the knowledge of God is directly in the center of this alleged dichotomy in Celsus' thought. The dichotomy, as it is defined, and perhaps resolved by Andresen, raises the significant question of the nature of Celsus' polemic. Is he simply

---

[9]Ibid., p. 59, "Kelsos wendet einen Wahrheitsbeweis an, der nicht aus den philosophischen Voraussetzungen seines Denkens abzuleiten ist. Daß er die Wahrheitsfrage von der Bestätigung durch geschichtlich bezeugte Beweise abhängig macht, is völlig unplatonisch. Nicht in der theoretischen Erkenntnis, im Logos, liegt die Wahrheit, sondern im empirischen Geschichtsbeweis."

[10]Ibid., p. 60, "erkennt man, daß zwischen ihnen ein spannungsreicher Gegensatz besteht."

[11]Ibid., p. 64, "Kelsos arbeitet also weniger mit einem religionsphilosophischen als mit einem geschichtskonstruktivem Argument."

biased, and does he, while unfairly accepting pagan inspiration, oracles, and approach to God-knowledge, reject that of the Christians because it is outside of his own cultural and historical experience? Or is there rather an integrating standard, or consistent criticism, which unifies his attack upon Christian doctrine and inspiration claims and justifies his acceptance of pagan ones? The answer to this question can only be obtained by an examination of Celsus' polemic, particularly as it relates to his understanding of the dependence of Christian doctrine upon inspiration and prophecy.

INSPIRATION IN CELSUS' POLEMIC

For Celsus, the issue must really be placed in the context of spiritual struggle. When one is discussing the knowledge of God, the question is not merely speculative but eminently practical; in a world filled with enticements, both material and spiritual, the danger of being misled into sorcery (γοητεία) rather than true divine knowledge, is always lurking. Like many of his contemporaries, Celsus is not asking whether prophetic experiences have occurred among the Christians,[12] but what sort they are, and from what spiritual source they come. One of his most significant and consistent charges against the Christians, therefore, is that of sorcery: the Christians, in their search for knowledge of God, have found sorcery and the daemonic, rather than prophecy and the divine.

For Celsus, all of the spiritual leaders of Christianity, from Moses to current teachers, are involved in sorcery in some form, and Christian doctrine, which claims to rest upon the inspired declarations of founders such as Moses and Jesus, betrays its occult source. Moses is one of the chief objects of the accusation of sorcery.[13] Aware of Moses' connection with Egypt, Celsus says that Moses acquired, in that center

---

[12] Even when Celsus questions the occurrence of Christian miracles, he asks only whether the events really happened or merely seemed to happen (cf. *Cels*. 1.41, 2.55).

[13] John G. Gager has surveyed Moses' reputation as a magician in the hellenistic world, in *Moses in Greco-Roman Paganism* (Nashville: Abingdon, 1972).

of the magical arts, a name for divine power.[14] The Jews, says Celsus, "worship angels and are addicted to sorcery of which Moses was their teacher" (*Cels.* 1.26). Moses, as the leader of the Jewish nation, and as its lawgiver and teacher, was fundamentally a γόης, and taught the Jews, not true knowledge of God, but sorcery and misguided doctrines that have a daemonic, rather than a divine source. Celsus says concerning the book of Genesis, "[The Jews] shamelessly undertook to trace their genealogy back to the first offspring of sorcerers and deceivers, invoking the witness of vague and ambiguous utterances concealed in some dark obscurity" (*Cels.* 4.33). The Jews, he says, "have no knowledge of the great God, but have been led on and deceived by Moses' sorcery and have learnt about that for no good purpose" (*Cels.* 5.41).

Jesus is an even better example, for Celsus, of a sorcerer who has deceived mankind with regard to the knowledge of God.[15] Born under questionable circumstances, he went to Egypt and "there tried his hand at certain magical powers on which the Egyptians pride themselves; he returned full of conceit because of these powers, and on account of them, gave himself the title of God" (*Cels.* 1.28). His wonders, which were really not all that extraordinary, were performed by magic and association with daemons. At his baptism, he conjured an apparition (φάσμα) of a dove (*Cels.* 1.39), his resurrection was witnessed only by "those who were deluded by the same sorcery" (*Cels.* 2.55), and after his resurrection, he produced "only a mental image (φαντασίαν) of the wounds he received on the cross" (*Cels.* 2.61). These, for Celsus, are not the products of divinity, but the works of a sorcerer (τὰ ἔργα τῶν γοήτων, *Cels.* 1.68). What is significant, however, about this particular γόης, according to Celsus, is that he has deluded humanity with his daemonic doctrine. The Christians, says Celsus, "were deceived, and accepted a doctrine harmful . . . to the life of mankind" (*Cels.* 1.26). Not only were the Christian founders entangled in sorcery, and their teaching consequently dangerous, but current

---

[14]*Cels.* 1.21, Τούτου οὖν, φασί, τοῦ λόγου τοῦ παρὰ τοῖς σοφοῖς ἔθνησι καὶ ἐλλογίμοις ἀνδράσιν ἐπακηκοὼς ὄνομα δαιμόνιον ἔσχε Μωϋσῆς.

[15]See Gallagher, *Divine Man or Magician?*

Christian prophecy, teaching, and practice are also ensnared in magic and involvement with the daemons. Contemporary Christians, says Celsus, get the power they seem to have "by pronouncing the names of certain daemons and incantations."[16] They are similar to the "begging priests of Cybele and soothsayers, and to worshippers of Mithras and Sabazius, and whatever else one might meet, apparitions of Hecate or of some other daemon or daemons."[17] Their doctrine, teachers, and leaders introduce, he says, like the Bacchic mysteries, "phantoms and terrors" (φάσματα καὶ τὰ δείματα, Cels. 4.10). Celsus says he has seen Christian elders with books containing the names of daemons and magical formulas, and cites as his prime example the Ophites, Christians who "court phantoms, deceivers, and sorcerers," and who depend for salvation upon the manipulation of daemonic "doorkeepers" with passwords (Cels. 7.40). These contemporary teachers, just like Moses and Jesus, because of their involvement with sorcery and the daemons, do not, and cannot, lead to the truth. Their prophets wander about making arrogant proclamations, but their sayings are,

> incomprehensible, incoherent, and utterly obscure utterances, the meaning of which no intelligent person could discover; for they are meaningless and nonsensical, and give a chance for any fool or sorcerer to take the words in whatever sense he likes.[18]

According to Celsus, such teachers blaspheme and mislead, and are quite ignorant of the truth about God (Cels. 7.42). Christians, rather than following the correct path to the great God, are continuously seeking new spiritual leaders, and as he says, "some have found as their leader

---

[16]Cels. 1.6, ὁ Κέλσος φησὶ δαιμόνων τινῶν ὀνόμασι καὶ κατακλήσεσι δοκεῖν ἰσχύειν Χριστιανούς.

[17]Cels. 1.9, Ἑκάτης ἢ ἄλλης δαίμονος ἢ δαιμόνων φάσμασιν. Hecate is particularly associated with φάσματα. Erwin Rohde, *Psyche: The Cult of Souls and Belief in Immortality among the Greeks.* (New York: Harcourt, Brace & Co., 1925), pp. 590-595.

[18]Cels. 7.9.

one teacher and daemon, and others another, for they go astray in evil ways and wander about in great darkness."[19]

Taken together, Celsus' criticisms amount to an assertion that, far from possessing divine inspiration, or having some special access to knowledge of God, Christian founders, prophets, and teachers are simply γόητες who have swindled the masses into believing what is an essentially blasphemous and ignorant doctrine. Where the apologists and intellectual Christians have attempted to rest the truth-claims of Christianity upon prophecy, Celsus rejects such claims as simple sorcery. The question remains, however, of the grounds for his rejection. As we have noted, it has long been recognized that Celsus accepts claims for pagan religion and cult which we have seen so violently rejected in the case of the Christians. Does he, as some have argued, play the part of the rationalizing critic in dealing with the Christians, and that of the staunch traditionalist, who conveniently overlooks the skeptical arguments when surveying the pagan past?[20] This may be so, but it would also seem likely that there should be a unifying theme in his treatment of claims to divine knowledge which makes sense of both sides of his argument. Such a theme can only be discovered in an examination of Celsus' views of the knowledge of God, demonology, and the dangers of entanglement in the earthly daemons.

THE KNOWLEDGE OF GOD

Celsus enunciates several methods to arrive at knowledge of God. Miura-Stange calls two of them "synthetic" and "intuitive." The first,

---

[19]*Cels.* 5.63, ἄλλοι ἄλλον διδάσκαλόν τε καὶ δαίμονα, κακῶς πλαζόμενοι καὶ καλινδούμενοι κατὰ σκότον πολύν.

[20]This seems to be the implication of Andresen's argument. Celsus accepts his own tradition because of his view of the historical value of the Greek past, and criticizes the Christians because they are outside of that tradition. This also seems to be the significance of Harold Remus' position concerning the "sociology of knowledge." (Remus, *Pagan and Christian*, particularly chapters 6 and 8). While Andresen and Remus, in different ways, convincingly assert the intellectual power of the past, and of social structures, it would seem helpful to extend their conclusions to determine the world-view which informs Celsus' reactionary approach to Christianity.

synthetic knowledge, is introduced in the context of negative theology characteristic of Middle Platonism.[21] Celsus cites the foundational text for the discussion of the knowledge of God, Plato's "Now to find the Maker and Father of this universe is difficult, and after finding him it is impossible to declare him to all men,"[22] and uses the negative attributes of ἄρρητος and ἀκατονόμαστος to describe God. He then outlines the three-fold method of Albinus: "that we might get some conception of the nameless First Being which manifests him either by synthesis with other things, or by analytical distinction from them, or by analogy"[23] This is an intellectual approach to understanding God, undertaken by training the mind to slough off the misconceptions engendered by the flesh and the world. It is a means to the ascetic goal of securing the rule of soul over body, and thus comprehending the things above.[24]

The intuitive method rests upon the kinship of the soul with God. According to Celsus, "there is something in man superior to the earthly part, which is related to God." The soul, which is συγγενὲς θεοῦ, "always longs for him to whom it is related, and they desire to hear something of him, and to be reminded (ἀναμιμνήσκεσθαι) about him" (Cels. 1.8). Celsus continues to quote Plato in saying, "All things centre in the King of all, and are for his sake, and he is the cause

---

[21]Ullmann asserts that Celsus does not speak in terms of Middle Platonic negative theology, but rather speaks of the manifest nature of God ("weltzugewandten Offenbarseins Gottes"). However, since Celsus cites the major loci of negative theology, and affirms the use of the methods of abstraction, it seems clear that he accepts it. W. Ullmann, "Die Bedeutung der Gotteserkenntnis für die Gesamtkonzeption von Celsus' Logos alethes," Studia Patristica 14, p. 185.

[22]Ti. 28 C, Cels. 7.42.

[23]Cels. 7.42, Albinus Epit. 10.5-6, Plato Resp. 508 B.

[24]Dörrie asserts that Celsus is completely rational in his approach to the knowledge of God. He says, "Bei diesem -- das muß unterstrichen werden -- deutet keine Silbe darauf hin, daß eine ekstatische unio mystica das Ziel aller philosophischen Bemühung sei: . . . von Anfang bis zu Ende ist diese Theologie an die Logik, an die λογισμοί, gebunden." This is, however, rather unlikely, particularly since Dörrie neglects Celsus' use of oracular knowledge, and his views of inspiration. One suspects that the modern categories of rational and irrational are not applicable, and indeed, not helpful, in dealing with antique thought. Heinrich Dörrie, "Die platonische Theologie des Kelsos," p. 38.

of all that is good. . . . The human soul, then, yearns to learn about these things."[25]   The kinship of the human soul to God, and its yearning to participate in the source of all, leads the soul to reach upward. After long striving, by methods including the synthetic, it shares in divinity, by virtue of its kinship and the contemplative quest. Celsus says, quoting Plato yet again, that knowledge of God, which is inexpressible, is awakened in the soul which is thus reaching upward: "the highest good cannot at all be expressed in words, but comes to us by long familiarity (ἐκ πολλῆς συνουσίας) and suddenly like a light in the soul kindled by a leaping spark."[26]   By συνουσία with God, made possible by συγγένεια, the soul shares in divine knowledge.

Celsus, however, is also willing to depend upon oracular sources for knowledge of God. Against Christian and Jewish claims of divine knowledge and revelation, he cites the oracular revelations given in the past, as well as those currently active. Animals, he says, "are so much nearer in communion with God," have divine knowledge, can foretell the future, and can convey that knowledge to human beings by divination.[27]

The stars as well give knowledge of God. Celsus calls the Chaldeans, famed for their astrology, "a race endowed with the highest inspiration" (*Cels.* 6.80). The stars and heavenly bodies, he says, are divine, and truly worthy of worship. They control and protect the fruitfulness of the earth, reveal God to man, and are "the clearest heralds of the powers above, the truly heavenly messengers" (*Cels.* 5.6).

The traditional oracles also provide knowledge of God. Against the Christian attempt to ground Christianity on the fulfillment of prophecy, and against the practice of prophecy current in his time,

---

[25] *Cels.* 6.18, Plato *Ep.* 2.312 E.

[26] *Cels.* 6.3. Plato *Ep.* 7.341 C.

[27] Celsus cites the evidence he knows concerning the knowledge of animals, but doesn't give a theory for the source of their divine knowledge. He implies that they have communion with God, even though they are irrational (*Cels.* 4.98). Origen cites the views of the Stoics, that the divinatory movements of animals are due to the daemons, and that of the Peripatetics, that the souls of animals are divine, with particularly low regard for the latter view. See Chadwick, *Contra Celsum*, p. 254, n. 3, and p. 261, n. 1.

Celsus complains, "The predictions of the Pythian priestess or of the priestesses of Dodona or of the Clarian Apollo or at Branchidae or at the shrine of Zeus Ammon, and of countless other prophets, are reckoned of no account, although it is probable that by them the whole world became inhabited" (*Cels.* 7.31). These oracular responses convey the knowledge of the future, and of God, by direct inspiration. Inspired people, possessed by divinity, speak from the oracles and shrines: "Why need I enumerate all the events which on the ground of oracular responses have been foretold with an inspired utterance (ἐνθέῳ φωνῇ) both by prophets and prophetesses and other inspired persons?" (*Cels.* 8.45).

The motivating theme in all these areas of God-knowledge is a Platonic one. Celsus says, in the quest for knowledge of God, "If you shut your eyes to the world of sense and look up with the mind, if you turn away from the flesh and raise the eyes of the soul, only so will you see God" (*Cels.* 7.36). Turning from the sensible world to the intelligible is the prime motif in his discussion of the knowledge of God. Whether it involves turning from the lowly angelic messengers of the Jews to the bright and divine heavenly bodies, from the sorcerers in the marketplace to the divinely inspired oracles, or from the flesh to συνουσία with God, it is a matter of fleeing the earthly regions and seeking the heavenly (*Cels.* 1.8).

Celsus thus does indeed affirm both 'philosophical' methods of God-knowledge as well as traditional popular ways. There is, however, no expressed conflict between the two in his thought. His criticisms of the Christians, and also of some manifestations of pagan practice, derive not so much from the methods they employ, but the results of those methods. The problem, for Celsus, is that the soul, as it yearns to ascend to God, remains too often trapped in flesh, and the earthly regions are filled with too many dangers waiting to turn it aside from its quest. The Christians, and the Jews as well, have fallen victim to these dangers, and succumbed to earthly daemons, who have deceived their ignorant victims in their search for the knowledge of God.

DEMONOLOGY

These dangers can be seen in Celsus' understanding of the intermediate beings who fill the void between man and God, the

daemons. Like most Platonists of his day, Celsus views the gap
between the lower region of matter and sense and the ineffable world of
the Good as filled with spiritual beings. These beings are above
humanity, since they are not bound to flesh, but, strictly speaking, are
not a part of God, since they are derivative.[28] To this daemonic realm
belongs the governance of the material world and the management of
human beings; the daemons are the ethereal civil service, overseeing
every facet of earthly affairs. Celsus, however, regards this realm with
an ambivalent eye; the upper reaches are pure, and sparkle with light
and clarity, but the lower realms, the areas with which humanity has
most to do, must be handled with caution.

Celsus says little of the highest realm of intermediary beings, but
mentions them enough to make clear that he considers them to be
divine and worthy of veneration. God, he says, created nothing mortal;
but there are immortal beings created by God, who are themselves
creators of everything else (*Cels*. 4.52). This is all he says concerning
these *demiurgoi*. It is probable, however, that these correspond to the
"most sacred and powerful parts" of the heavens, the stars.[29] These fall
into the rank of gods (*Cels*. 5.2), and according to Celsus, they are
"truly heavenly messengers," who control all those lesser
meteorological phenomena which are worshiped by the Jews. Celsus
does not class them with the daemons who are of a somewhat more
equivocal character, and asserts that they "prophesy so clearly and
distinctly to everyone," and are the "clearest heralds of the powers
above."[30]

There is another circle of beings in Celsus' heavenly hierarchy,
however, which is directly involved in the management of the peoples
of the world, the *Volksdämonen*.[31] To these spiritual intermediaries is
given oversight of each human nation. According to Celsus, the
differences between peoples are due to the fact that "from the beginning

---

[28]Plato *Symp*. 202 D 13, "Everything that is daemonic, is intermediate
between God and mortal." Cited by Dodds, *Pagan and Christian*, p. 37. According
to Dodds, "in the second century after Christ it was an expression of a truism."

[29]So Miura-Stange, *Celsus und Origenes*, p. 89; cf. *Cels*. 5.6, Plato *Ti*. 41 C.

[30]*Cels*. 5.6, τοὺς δ' οὕτως καὶ λαμπρῶς ἅπασι προφητεύοντας . . .
τοὺς φανερωτάτους τῶν ἄνω κήρυκας.

[31]Andresen, *Logos und Nomos*, p. 198.

the different parts of the earth were allotted to different authorities" (*Cels.* 5.25). Each nation, therefore, ought to please its overseer in maintaining its traditional practices, both in law and religion. The overseer in this sense corresponds to the satrap or procurator of an emperor (or, from the proper angle, the human satrap is a reflection of the heavenly overseer) who, under the ruler's *monarchia*, governs within his own realm. These ἐπόπτοι play a significant role in Celsus' attack upon the Christians, for they sanction a connection between traditional piety and political conformity, and make it clear that *stasis* in matters of religion carries over into both human and celestial society.[32]

There are also a host of other spiritual beings who fill up the lower ranks of the spiritual bureaucracy. Celsus argues, against the Christians who refuse to honor the daemons, that one cannot lead a normal life on this earth without encroaching upon the domain of some daemon. He says, "Either we ought not to live at all anywhere on earth and not to enter this life, or if we do enter this life under these conditions, we ought to give thanks to the daemons who have been allotted control over earthly things" (*Cels.* 8.33). Like Tertullian, Celsus thinks that souls are allotted to daemons at birth,[33] and various daemons govern marriage, the begetting of children, and "anything else in life" (*Cels.* 8.55). Celsus, though not quite sure about the exact names and number of these beings, records that the Egyptians divide the body into at least thirty-six parts, each with its own daemon. When the Christians eat food, taste fruits, drink wine or water, "are they not receiving each of these from certain daemons, among whom the administration of each of these has been divided?" (*Cels.* 8.28). Celsus says, "in these matters, even including the very least, there is a being to whom authority has been given" (*Cels.* 8.58).

The Danger of Entanglement. The ubiquity of the daemons and their close association with humanity provides the basis for Celsus' concern for the proper exercise of religion and the correct path to true knowledge

---

[32]See Andresen, *Logos und Nomos*, particularly pp. 189-238.

[33]*Cels.* 8.34. Tertullian argues that because of pagan natal ceremonies, an evil daemon is attached to the soul at birth (*De an.* 39). Plutarch speaks of daemons which accompany their souls from birth into the after life (*De gen.* 592-593).

of God. The soul is always in danger, for Celsus, of being side-tracked by fascination with the lower daemons and the material order with which they are associated, and of being thus deceived and turned aside from its ascent to God. This is clear in his discussion of the daemons and the proper way to venerate them.

Celsus affirms that the daemons are to be worshiped. After all, they, like everything else, are within the realm of the great God, and worship given to them ultimately redounds to his glory. Celsus thus cannot see the cogency of the Christian attack on idolatry, nor their concern that God alone be worshiped. If the popular divinities are daemons, as the Christians say, "obviously these too belong to God, and we ought to believe them and sacrifice to them according to the laws, and pray to them that they may be kindly disposed" (Cels. 8.27).

However, with regard to the worship of daemons, Celsus is somewhat less enthusiastic than he is in his description of the stars and heavenly bodies. Daemons are rather equivocal and untrustworthy beings, and when blasphemed, he says, they can be positively inimical:

> How many, on the other hand, have insulted the temples and have at once been caught? For some have been overcome by madness on the spot; others have declared what they had done; others have become bound by incurable diseases. Some have even been destroyed by a deep voice from the actual shrines.[34]

It is necessary, therefore, to honor the daemons, not so much because of their glory, but in order to retain their favor, and in order to live untroubled in this life and flesh which they control. "We ought to give thanks," says Celsus, "to the daemons who have been allotted control over earthly things . . . that we may obtain their goodwill towards us" (Cels. 8.33). It makes good sense to honor those beings who can either favor us or hurt us, and it is good spiritual politics to venerate them, "so that we can be in good health rather than be ill, and have good rather than bad luck, and be delivered from tortures and punishment."[35]

---

[34]Cels. 8.45.

[35]Cels. 8.58. According to Maximus of Tyre, the varieties of daemonic dispositions is endless: "one is terrible, another kind, one civil, another warlike - - as many natures of men, so many also of daemons." Max. Diss. 14.8.

This honor, however, should never be an end in itself. "We ought," says Celsus, "to pay formal acknowledgement to them, in so far as this is expedient -- for reason does not require us to do this in all cases" (*Cels.* 8.62). These lower daemons are ambiguous beings, tied to the material order, and while they ought to be honored for 'expediency's' sake, they must never be the goal of the soul's yearning and fascination.

The problem has to do with their nature. Although δαίμων is a neutral term, and has a consistently evil connotation only in Christian writings, for Celsus, the daemons of the lower region are not to be trusted. He is evidently aware of the categories (γένη) in the *Timaeus* myth,[36] and carefully distinguishes between the gods of the heavens, the stars and planets, and the lower daemons. Celsus asks the Jews and Christians about their attraction to heavenly messengers, and says, "and if it is certain angels of which you speak, whom do you mean by them, gods or some other kind of being? You presumably mean some other kind -- the daemons" (*Cels.* 5.2). In his distinction, θεοὺς ἢ ἄλλο τι γένος, he is drawing from Plato's four classes (γένη) of beings. The first of these is the divine *genos*, the star-gods, οὐράνιον θεῶν γένος, created from fire, containing the "intelligence of the Supreme" (Plato *Ti.* 40 A). This is what Celsus has in mind when he asks the Christians, τίνας τούτους λέγετε, θεοὺς ἢ ἄλλο τι γένος; and he concludes that they mean "some other kind (γένος)," that is, the daemons.[37] The daemons are thus not to be classed with the heavenly messengers who prophesy clearly and distinctly, but rather belong to the less trustworthy class surrounding the earth. These beings, says Celsus, are not to be trifled with. They were cast down from heaven for the sin of arrogance, and were punished by being sent down to earth.[38] They are now the jailers of this earthly prison, to which human souls have also been consigned (*Cels.* 8.53). They are concerned only with the material, and even the good they do is associated only with the body, not the soul. Celsus says,

> For perhaps we ought not to disbelieve wise men who say that most of the earthly daemons are absorbed with created things,

---

[36]*Ti.* 39 E - 41 E.
[37]*Cels.* 5.2, ἄλλο τι ὡς εἰκός, τοὺς δαίμονας.

and are riveted to blood and burnt-offerings and magical
enchantments, and bound to other things of this sort, and can
do nothing better than healing the body and predicting the
coming fortune of men and cities, and that all their knowledge
and power concerns merely mortal activities.[39]

Here Celsus' demonology makes contact with his understanding of
the knowledge of God. He gives a warning concerning the daemons:

We must however, be careful about this, lest by association
with these beings anyone should become absorbed in the
healing with which they are concerned, and by becoming a
lover of the body and turning away from higher things should
be held down without realizing it.[40]

There are two facets of this warning which relate directly to his
understanding of the proper method of acquiring God-knowledge. He is
concerned about the problem of association (συνουσία), and the
problem of turning (ἀποστρέφω).

As we have noted, Celsus feels that one means of acquiring
knowledge is by "familiarity." One of the central passages for his
understanding of God-knowledge is his quotation of Plato, who says,
"the highest good cannot at all be expressed in words, but comes to us
by long familiarity (ἀλλ' ἐκ πολλῆς συνουσίας) and suddenly like
a light in the soul kindled by a leaping spark."[41] Because of
συγγένεια θεοῦ, the soul longs for God, and by the discipline of the
philosophical life, can participate in God by συνουσία. This same
συνουσία, however, can also be exercised with the daemons. As
noted above, Celsus warns, "We must however be careful about this,
lest by association (συνὼν) with these beings anyone should become
absorbed in the healing with which they are concerned."[42] *Synousia* of

---

[38]*Cels.* 6.42. For sources, see Chadwick, *Contra Celsum*, pp. 358-9.

[39]*Cels.* 8.60.

[40]Ibid.

[41]*Cels.* 6.3, Plato *Ep.* 7 341 C.

[42]*Cels.* 8.60, ἐκεῖνο μέντοι φυλακτέον, ὅπως μή τις συνὼν τούτοις τῇ
θεραπείᾳ τῇ αὐτὰ συντακῇ.

this sort leads not to knowledge or love of God, but Celsus says, to love of the body and captivity in the lower world. One becomes "held down in the place of oblivion,"[43] trapped and deceived into love of material things by an attraction to the extraordinary manifestations of the therapeutic and divinatory powers of the daemons.

There is also a false 'turning.' Celsus told us that the way to true knowledge of God was to "shut your eyes to the world of sense and look up with the mind, [to] turn away from the flesh (σαρκὸς ἀποστραφέντες) and raise the eyes of the soul" (*Cels.* 7.36). However, by unwise association with the daemons, Celsus says that the unsuspecting soul can, "by becoming a lover of the body and turning away from higher things . . . be held down without realizing it" (*Cels.* 8.60). Here intercourse with the daemons and their works, which might, in a temporal sense, be quite beneficial, leads to τῶν κρειττόνων ἀποστραφεὶς, a turning, not away from the flesh and towards God, but away from the superior things to the flesh and the lower order, which again, results in captivity in this "place of oblivion." Therefore, when according the daemons the honor which is "expedient," one must be very careful not to be attracted, and thus trapped, in their realm. While the daemons must be placated to maintain a trouble-free life on earth, one must not become unnecessarily entangled with them. This entanglement, which can take the soul unaware, results in an unknowing captivity.

After asserting that the daemons ought to be honored, therefore, Celsus gives the antidote to their influence:

> But we ought never to forsake God at all, neither by day nor by night, neither in public nor in private. In every word and deed, and in fact, both with them [the daemons] and without them, let the soul be continually directed towards God.[44]

---

[43]*Cels.* 8.60, λήθη κατασχεθῇ, my translation.

[44]*Cels.* 8.60, θεοῦ δὲ οὐδαμῇ οὐδαμῶς ἀπολειπτέον οὔτε μεθ' ἡμέραν οὔτε νύκτωρ οὔτ' ἐς κοινὸν οὔτ' ἰδίᾳ λόγῳ τε ἐν παντὶ καὶ ἔργῳ διηνεκῶς, ἀλλά γε καὶ μετὰ τῶνδε καὶ χωρὶς ἡ ψυχὴ ἀεὶ τετάσθω πρὸς τὸν θεόν. Andresen sees this passage as evidence of the dichotomy in Celsus' thought, and argues that with the words "neither by day nor by night,

The soul of the wise person is always on guard against daemonic influence because it is always turned towards God. The wise man therefore can honor the daemons, grant them their due, and even partake of their material benefits without fear of entanglement, if the eyes of the soul are always lifted away from this world of sense, and turned towards God. Such a person, however, has less and less to do with the daemons and their world, as his soul rises to God. In this sense Celsus can say that magic, the domain of the daemons, has no effect on people so warned. A certain Egyptian, he says, "told him that magical arts were effective with uneducated people and with men of depraved moral character, but with people who had studied philosophy they were not able to have any effect, because they were careful to lead a healthy way of life" (*Cels.* 6.41).

The same sort of concern is evident in Philostratus' presentation of Apollonius of Tyana. His "healthy way of life," his asceticism, his abstention from animal foods, and his devotion to spiritual truth resulted in power over daemons and their apparitions and an unusual view of future events as well as divine truth. For Celsus, the "healthy way" consists of the proper orientation of the soul to God, and the awareness of the captivating influence of the daemons.

Christian Entanglement. "If you look for some one to lead you along this path," says Celsus, "you must flee from the deceivers and sorcerers who court phantoms" (*Cels.* 7.36). This, according to Celsus, is exactly what the Jews and the Christians have not done. They have rejected both the trustworthy heavenly messengers and the wise men who have true knowledge of God, and instead, followed sorcerers and sought out phantoms. When he chastises the Jews for worshiping, not the heavenly gods, but ἄλλο τι γένος . . . τοὺς δαίμονας, he says that they prefer "beings which are alleged to draw near to people blinded in darkness somewhere as a result of black magic, or who have

---

neither in public nor in private," Celsus is making his distinction between official and personal piety. However, this places a great amount of weight on this expression, and does not do justice to what seems to be the point of the passage. Celsus' expressed concern is that the soul be directed towards God, and placed in the context of his warning of 8.60, the meaning becomes clear. Andresen, *Logos und Nomos*, p. 60.

dreams of obscure phantoms."[45]   This is his opinion of the Jewish-
Christian claim to prophecy and divine inspiration: their prophets and
founders have actually been consorting with daemons, and their
prophecies are daemonic phantasms which display an inordinate love of
the flesh.

Celsus gives some characteristics of the type of doctrine, which, in
its reliance upon inspiration, has been waylaid in its attempt to see
God. First of all, those who consort with daemons can indeed
prophesy, at least if this is understood simply as predicting the future.
This, moreover, is a characteristic function of the daemons; predicting
the future is an appropriately earthy activity, for, as Celsus says, the
daemons only predict the "coming fortune of men and cities" (*Cels.*
8.60). This is no great feat; Celsus says, "they can do nothing better."
According to Celsus, "All their knowledge and power concerns merely
mortal activities" (*Cels.* 8.60).

Secondly, prophecy of this type, says Celsus, is characterized by
ambiguity and obscurity. As we have seen, the charge of ambiguity
was a common one in discussions of prophecy. Plutarch noted
contemporary mistrust of ambiguous oracles, Lucian saw it as a sign of
quackery, and it was often viewed as an indication of the presence of
some perverting or confusing influence.[46] Celsus turns this charge on
Christian prophecy, and cites as an example the wandering prophets of
Palestine, of whom, he says, he has first-hand knowledge:

> There are many . . . who are nameless, who prophesy at the
> slightest excuse for some trivial cause both inside and outside
> temples; and there are some who wander about begging and
> roaming around cities and military camps; and they pretend to
> be moved as if giving some oracular utterance . . . they . . .
> add incomprehensible, incoherent, and utterly obscure
> utterances, the meaning of which no intelligent person could
> discover; for they are meaningless and nonsensical, and give a

---

[45] *Cels.* 5.6, τοὺς μὲν ἐν σκότῳ που ἐκ γοητείας οὐκ ὀρθῆς
τυφλώττουσιν ἢ δι' ἀμυδρῶν φασμάτων ὀνειρώττουσιν ἐγχρίμπτειν
λεγομένους εὖ μάλα θρησκεύειν.

[46] Plutarch *De Pyth. or.* 407 A, Lucian *Alex.* 10, Philostratus *VA* 2.37.

chance for any fool or sorcerer to take the words in whatever sense he likes.[47]

Whether or not this fragment provides an accurate picture of any group within Christianity, it is clear that Celsus intends to discredit all Jewish and Christian prophecy claims with this caricature.[48] That this is the case is evident by the context; the next fragment begins, "those who base their defense of the doctrine of Christ upon the prophets have not a word to say if one points out some utterance about God which is wicked, or disgraceful, or impure, or abominable."[49] The polemical concern is paramount: such charlatans are the perfect example of the types of inspiration claims made by the Christians, which result in incoherent and ambiguous oracles useful only for sorcery. This emphasis upon ambiguity and obscurity can then be seen, for Celsus, in a comparison between Jewish-Christian prophecy, and the more trustworthy revelations from the heavens. Celsus characterizes the revelations of Moses as ἀμυδρὰς, ἀμφιβόλους φωνὰς, and ἐν σκότῳ που κρυφίους (Cels. 4.33), while the true heavenly messengers prophesy ἐναργῶς καὶ λαμπρῶς and are τοὺς φανερωτάτους τῶν ἄνω κήρυκας (Cels. 5.6).

More importantly, another characteristic of this type of daemonic inspiration is the appearance of φάσμα and φαντασία. We have seen that in texts such as the Life of Apollonius phantasms and apparitions serve to indicate the presence of confused, illicit, or magical prophecy, and are contrasted to the wisdom possessed by the true prophet, who does not depend upon spirits or apparitions. Celsus likewise, in his assertion that the Christians are involved with earthly daemons, points to their reliance upon visions, phantasms, and apparitions. When the Jews turn from the "truly heavenly messengers," he says, what they get are "beings which are alleged to draw to people blinded in darkness somewhere as a result of black magic" (Cels. 5.6).

---

[47]Cels. 7.9. This language is similar to Lucian's derogatory characterization of Alexander's teacher Cocconas, who produced διττούς τινας καὶ ἀμφιβόλους καὶ λοξοὺς χρησμοὺς συγγράφων. Lucian, Alex. 11.

[48]For literature, see Chadwick, Contra Celsum, p.403, n. 6.

[49]Cels. 7.12. See Bader's juxtaposition of fragments. Robert Bader, Der Alethes Logos des Kelsos, pp. 177-179.

Turning to the daemons results in dealings with nightly visitors, and the appearance of φάσματα. These apparitions are one of the major characteristics of involvement with the daemons. Celsus gives a classic description of γοητεία when, in comparing Jesus to Egyptian magicians, he cites,

> the works of sorcerers who profess to do wonderful miracles ... who for a few obols make known their sacred lore in the middle of the market-place and drive daemons out of men and blow away diseases and invoke the souls of heroes, displaying expensive banquets and dining-tables and cakes and dishes which are non-existent, and who make things move as though they were alive although they are not really so, but only appear as such in the imagination.[50]

One should not consider those who can make such φαντασίας φαινόμενα to be divine, says Celsus, but rather ἀνθρώπων πονηρῶν καὶ κακοδαιμόνων.[51]

It is on the basis of φάσμα and φαντασία that Christianity has been founded, according to Celsus. We have seen that he considers Moses and the prophets to be sorcerers who are involved with daemons, but Celsus asserts that Jesus as well falls into the class of ἀνθρώπων πονηρῶν καὶ κακοδαιμόνων. Jesus' alleged miracles were simply the product of magic, and the events of his life upon which the Christians depend for proof of his divinity were merely φάσματα. The bird at the baptism was only a φάσμα, says Celsus, (*Cels.* 1.41), and the only proof for the resurrection was, "a hysterical female, as you say, and perhaps some other one of those who were deluded by the same sorcery, who either dreamt in a certain state of mind and through

---

[50]*Cels.* 1.68, καὶ ὡς ζῷα κινόυντων οὐκ ἀληθῶς ὄντα ζῷα ἀλλὰ μέχρι φαντασίας φαινόμενα τοιαῦτα.

[51]Celsus does use the term φάσμα positively, in connection with the traditional oracles (τοῖς δ᾽ ἐναργῆ παρέστη φάσματα), but this is still in the context of contact with the daemons, and consequently his warning against too close contact with the daemons (*Cels.* 8.60) applies even in this positive context. To the φάσματα of the Christians he opposes the actual appearances of the gods (*Cels.* 7.36), and of Asclepius: *Cels.* 3.24, οὐ φάσμα αὐτὸ τοῦτο ἀλλὰ θεραπεύοντα καὶ εὐεργετοῦντα καὶ τὰ μέλλοντα προλέγοντα.

wishful thinking had a hallucination due to some mistaken notion
(δόξη πεπλανημένη φαντασιωθείς, *Cels.* 2.55)." The wounds
of the cross, produced by Jesus after the resurrection, were likewise,
says Celsus, only φαντασίας. The Christians, building on this
foundation, are like "those in the Bacchic mysteries who introduce
phantoms and terrors (τὰ φάσματα καὶ τὰ δείματα, *Cels.*
4.10)."

The Christians, therefore, are prime examples of those who have
incautiously consorted with daemons. In seeking revelation and
inspiration, their prophets and founders have found, not the knowledge
of God, but a false and fleshly doctrine which is the tool of the daemons
to entrap them in the lower regions. They have rejected the proper
guides on the way of truth, and in that rejection have followed those
who only deceive and enslave them.

It is in this context that Celsus' recourse to the Ophites makes sense.
Origen protested that Celsus, who claimed to "know all," should know
better than to lay the doctrines of the Ophites at the feet of the
orthodox. Indeed, many scholars in the past have not known quite what
to do with Celsus' use of the Ophite diagram,[52] and it has often been
viewed as evidence of the fluid social character of Christianity.[53]
However, Celsus is not so much concerned with providing an accurate
portrait of Christianity as he is with obtaining ammunition for his
polemical task. For this purpose the case of the Ophites and other
Gnostics is particularly well-suited; from his information, Celsus finds
them to be perfect examples of those who have turned to the daemons
and become entangled.

According to Celsus, the Ophites and other Gnostics have a doctrine
of the ascent of the soul back to God through the realms which encircle
the earth. Unlike the Mithraic mysteries, which speak of the travel of

---

[52]For example, Andresen sees it as fodder for Celsus' satire, while Heinrich
Dörrie says that Celsus doesn't know or care about the difference between the
Gnostics and the Christians, and that the treatment of the Ophites is simply a
snide remark on the periphery of his argument. Andresen, *Logos und Nomos*, p.
176, and Dörrie, "Die platonische Theologie des Kelsos," p. 33.

[53]For example, Walter Bauer, *Orthodoxy and Heresy in Earliest Christianity*,
2nd German edition, trans. by Philadelphia Seminar on Christian Origins, ed.
Robert A. Kraft and Gerhardt Krodel (Philadelphia: Fortress, 1971), p. 236, n. 13.

the soul to heaven by way of the planets (reflecting sound Platonic doctrine, according to Celsus), the Gnostic teachings make the soul do business with wicked daemonic guardians.[54] According to the Ophites, the soul must journey through realms of archontic angels (*Cels.* 6.27). At death the soul is surrounded by seven angels of light and seven archons, the chief of which is the "accursed God." It passes through the regions of these archons, who have the shape of lion, bull, serpent, eagle, bear, dog, and ass. This journey through hostile territory is accomplished by the recitation of passwords which procure passage through the "eternally chained gates of the Archons."[55] In Celsus' formula of salvation, therefore, the Ophites, and by extension, the Christians, fall into the category of those who, "seeking a guide on this path," have not fled from deceivers and sorcerers, but instead "court phantoms, deceivers, and sorcerers," and have "wretchedly learnt by heart the names of the doorkeepers" (*Cels.* 7.40).

The Problem of Guides. The issue, for Celsus, is really one of spiritual guides.[56] The road to divine knowledge, the path of the soul to God, is a perilous one, and one which is beyond the independent capabilities of most people. "The way of truth," says Celsus, "is sought by seers and philosophers, and . . . Plato knew that it is impossible for all men to travel it" (*Cels.* 7.42). The problem is how to find guidance on this way, and for Celsus, the Christians have made the mistake of following the wrong guides. We have seen that he considers Moses and Jesus to have been hopelessly entangled in the lower daemons, and consequently they constitute guides of the worst type: "The goatherds and shepherds who followed Moses as their leader were deluded by clumsy deceits" (*Cels.* 1.23). The Christians have been so deluded by their dependence upon these false guides, says Celsus, that they might more likely find the truth with a toss of the dice (*Cels.* 6.11).

---

[54]Cf. *Cels.* 6.21 and *Cels.* 6.22. Celsus alludes to Plato *Phdr.* 248 C - E, and *Ti.* 41 D - 42 E. Chadwick, *Contra Celsum*, 6. 21, n. 11.

[55]This is according to Origen. *Cels.* 6.31.

[56]See Andresen, *Logos und Nomos*, pp. 131-135.

The issue does not concern the reality of inspiration, however, but rather the misleading influence of the daemons. The trustworthy guides on the path to truth are indeed inspired men, but their inspiration is divine, and free of the deceptive roadblocks of the earthly daemons. These inspired men have been successful, where the Christians have failed, in raising the eyes of the soul towards God.

Seers and philosophers are the ones who travel the ἀληθείας ὁδός, and these great sages are θεῖοι ἄνδρες (*Cels.* 7.42). Chief among these is Plato, but also to be included are the poets and the great figures of the Greek past, including Orpheus, Anaxarchus, Epictetus, and others.[57] The significance of the inspiration of these men is that they are θεῖοι, not δαιμόνιοι, at least in the earthly sense of the term. The contact of the soul with the divine is at the heart of Celsus' epistemology, and he therefore considers those who have arrived at the truth to be influenced by the divine. God, says Celsus, wants to give us knowledge of himself for our salvation,[58] and thus has been making himself known throughout human history. Celsus is therefore willing to grant to the Christians that "some spirit came down from God to foretell the divine truths. . . . It was because men of ancient times were touched by this spirit that they proclaimed many excellent doctrines."[59] The Christians however, who follow the daemons, cannot understand such doctrines, because they have been "entirely lamed and mutilated in souls and live for the body which is a dead thing" (*Cels.* 7.45). True inspiration is the pure contact of the soul with God which is above the corrupting and restraining influence of the daemons.

---

[57]See Andresen's treatment of the παλαιός λόγος, *Logos und Nomos*, pp. 108-135.

[58]*Cels.* 4.7. Cf. Andresen, ibid.

[59]*Cels.* 7.45, καὶ πνεῦμα εἴ τι οἴεσθε κατιὸν ἐκ θεοῦ προαγγέλλειν τὰ θεῖα, τοῦτ᾿ ἂν εἴη τὸ πνεῦμα τὸ ταῦτα κηρύττον, οὗ δὴ πλησθέντες ἄνδρες παλαιοὶ πολλὰ κἀγαθὰ ἤγγειλαν.

CELSUS AND HIS CONTEXT

The type of argument on inspiration which Celsus has put forward against the Christians is perhaps more understandable when the context of the apologetic struggle is recalled. The Christian apologists had been asserting that Jesus of Nazareth was the incarnate logos of God, and arguing that the proof of this was to be found in the prophets of the Old Testament and the ethical and spiritual power of Christianity. Beyond that, Justin had argued that this logos had always been seeking to communicate with humanity, but that the evil daemons had succeeded in blinding all but a few to its message. This argument of Justin puts Celsus' position in a somewhat sharper light.[60]

Justin, in his appeal to the "pious and truth-loving" emperor (1 *ap.* 1), asserts that the persecution of the Christians is the work, not of piety and reason, but of the evil daemons. He says, "Such things, we are convinced, are brought about by the evil demons, the ones who demand sacrifices and service from men who live irrationally" (1 *ap.* 12). These daemons have succeeded in corrupting the logos, perverting its message, and so imitating it in idolatry, that they have effectively prevented humanity from coming to a knowledge of God (1 *ap.* 54-56). The daemons' corrupting power is ineffective, however against the triumphant power of the cross, but even after the incarnation, crucifixion, and resurrection, they carry on their mission of holding humanity down in the earthly regions, the realm of passion and irrationality. Only the Christians, protected by the cleansing and sealing power of baptism, are free from their influence, and can be properly called no longer children of "necessity and ignorance, but of free choice and knowledge" (1 *ap.* 61).

The power of the daemons to restrain mankind in irrationality and fleshliness extends, for Justin, throughout the Greek tradition, and there exist only glimmers of the logos in the Greek past. Most of Greek literature and tradition, particularly that having to do with the gods and

---

[60]Andresen has argued persuasively that Celsus is replying to Justin. *Logos und Nomos*, pp. 308-372.

their lascivious behavior, is due to the corrupting influence of the daemons. This power to hold the human race in ignorance continues to the present day, moreover, and extends even to the emperor:

> We warn you in advance to be careful, lest the demons whom we have attacked should deceive you and prevent your completely grasping and understanding what we say. For they struggle to have you as their slaves and servants.[61]

The purpose of the daemons, says Justin, is to prevent human beings from achieving true knowledge of God, and they do this, "now by manifestations in dreams, now by magic tricks, they get hold of all who do not struggle to their utmost for their own salvation" (1 *ap*. 14). This is his understanding of daemonic activity:

> For those who are called demons strive for nothing else than to draw men away from God who made them and from Christ his First-begotten. Those who cannot rise above the earth they have nailed down by the worship of earthly things and the works of men's hands. They even push back those who aim at the contemplation of things divine, unless their thinking is prudent and pure and their life free from passion, and drive them into ungodliness.[62]

Those who are attempting to raise their souls toward God are thus waylaid by the daemons, who entrap all but the most disciplined, and restrain their souls in the earthly and fleshly regions.

The similarity to the language of Celsus is striking. Justin argues that the Greeks have been deceived by daemons, who have intercepted the souls of the unwary as they have attempted to rise to knowledge of God. As we have seen, this is the same argument which Celsus makes against the Christians as they claim to have pure knowledge of God based upon inspiration and prophecy. Whether or not Celsus is responding directly to Justin, the point at issue is the very practical matter of how one deals with the powerful spiritual forces surrounding

---

[61] Justin 1 *ap*. 14.
[62] 1 *ap*. 58.

this prison-house, and the question of which tradition most potently enables one to lift the soul to its heavenly home. The Christians have argued that only by the breakthrough of the logos, first in the ancient prophets, and then fully in the incarnation, is the restraining power of the daemons broken. Celsus takes up this pressing religious question. He grants the power of the daemons, but argues that it is the Christians, not the Greeks, who have fallen prey to their wicked influence.

The tension which many scholars have seen to exist in Celsus' treatment of inspiration, prophecy, and the extraordinary can now be approached more clearly. As we have seen, Andresen has argued that there is an inner dichotomy in Celsus' view of these things, and that his acceptance of wonders, inspiration, and daemon-worship is grudgingly given only on the basis of the concept of history. Only because these things have been grounded in the tradition, and because their occurrence is attested by the authority of the past, is Celsus willing to allow them, even though they contradict his basic philosophical position. On the other hand, according to Andresen, he criticizes the Christian claims on the basis that they stand outside of the ancient logos.

It is now clear, however, that there exists in Celsus' thought not so much an inner tension, resolved by a philosophical concept of history, but rather an inner continuity, preserved by a view of the cosmos and an approach to the knowledge of God. Celsus possesses a criterion for judging claims to divine intimacy, which, while leveled at the Christians, is applied to all religious phenomena of his day. The question is whether those claiming spiritual power have been snared by the intervening influence of the earthly daemons, or have succeeded in rising above them. Celsus accepts popular religion when its practice is "expedient" and reasonable; but he is equally willing to criticize it when it goes beyond those bounds into love of the flesh and the daemons. The fragment which Andresen uses to show the dichotomy in Celsus' thought between public and private religion demonstrates not discontinuity, but the homogeneity of the application of this point of view:

But we ought never to forsake God at all, neither by day nor by night, neither in public nor in private. In every word and deed,

and in fact, both with them [the daemons] and without them, let
the soul be continually directed towards God.[63]

This concern places Celsus squarely within the ranks of his
contemporaries. He cannot be seen as the last holdout of hellenic
rationalism, combating the growing foes of superstition and fideism,
nor as a schizophrenic, whose heart-felt beliefs contradict his
intellectual viewpoints. Rather he shares the common religious
concerns of his day, and meets head-on the challenges set forth by the
Christians. The Christians raise questions about the source of religious
knowledge and the nature of spiritual power, and these are the central
issues which Celsus takes up. If Peter Brown is correct in his
assessment of the development of Late Antique thought, it is clear that
Celsus must be seen within this development. According to Brown,
the Late Antique person was concerned with the sources of spiritual
power, and this included misgivings about the influence of the
daemons. He says,

> Late Antique thought stressed their ambiguous and anomalous
> status . . . [the presence of the daemons] in the "earthly
> regions" introduced a constant element of indeterminacy and
> confusion into the clear structure that linked rightful agents of
> the supernatural to their heavenly source.[64]

This is the concern of Celsus, and he meets the Christian challenge in a
way characteristic of the Late Antique person who, according to Brown,
"faced the supernatural with a set of cosmic beliefs that had filled his
mind with a meticulous and exacting questionnaire as to the alternative
sources of any manifestation of the supernatural."[65] The question of
prophecy and inspiration, for both parties in this struggle, consists of
the fundamental question of the sources of spiritual power and truth,
freedom from external, often inimical, forces, and the unrestrained
journey of the soul to God.

---

[63]*Cels.* 8.63, Andresen, *Logos und Nomos*, p. 60.
[64]Brown, *Making of Late Antiquity*, p. 20.
[65]Ibid., p. 19.

Chapter 5

"Clear Mental Vision:"

Origen's Divine Proof

> The gospel has a proof which is peculiar to
> itself, and which is more divine than a Greek
> proof based on dialectical argument. This
> more divine demonstration the apostle calls a
> 'demonstration of the Spirit and of power' --
> of spirit because of the prophecies and
> especially those which refer to Christ, which
> are capable of convincing any one who reads
> them. *Origen Cels.1.2.*

With such a beginning, Origen places himself squarely within the
preceding apologetic tradition. Generations before, Justin Martyr
protested, "We do not trust in mere hearsay, but are forced to believe
those who prophesied these things before they happened" (1 *apol.* 30).
The Christian apologists had long defended their faith on the grounds
that the truths of Christianity had perennially been preached by men
inspired by God.

For Origen, however, the time had passed when a simple assertion of
the prophecies and their fulfillment would do. Celsus, and it may be
assumed, many others by Origen's time, failed to see the force of the
eagerly promoted fulfillments. While acknowledging that Moses and
the other prophets may have had spiritual experiences, Celsus charged
that they were actually consorting with daemons who were attempting
to keep them bound to the lower world of sense and matter. The

prophets were therefore under the influence not of God or a holy spirit, but of daemons and lower spiritual beings, and thus should be considered sorcerers rather than prophets.

The issue between Christian and pagan is thus one of spiritual discernment and spiritual warfare. The earlier apologists had argued that Greek culture, for the most part, lay under the deceptive sway of the daemons. Celsus responded by arguing that the Christians are the ones who, with their love of prophecy and visions, have been led astray by the lower order of daemons, and deceived into thinking that they possess divine truth. The debate over prophecy thus stands directly in the center of the apologetic struggle. It provides the battle-ground for the question of the knowledge of God, and the practical question of spiritual power and freedom. In Celsus' offensive, the attack focused on the character of the prophets' lives and the nature of their experience. It is here, as well, that Origen's defense centers. He is out to prove that the prophets' inspiration was from God, and their knowledge divine.

This question, as it presents itself in *Against Celsus*, is one which has not been closely examined by modern scholars. As we have indicated, Celsus has usually been examined with regard to his place in the debate between rationality and faith, while his spiritual concerns have been overlooked. In the case of Origen, there has been a long and voluminous debate about the spiritual character, or lack thereof, of Origen's system, but little concern for this issue within the context of apologetic. As Karl Pichler has pointed out, there has been a wealth of *Kelsos-Forschung* and a dearth of *Contra-Celsum-Forschung*.[1] Origen's views on prophecy have usually been treated in relation to his exegesis or his mysticism,[2] and his assertion that the Scriptures are inspired is usually considered significant in that it provides a warrant for allegory. Henri de Lubac thus cites Gustave Bardy to the effect that "Origène ne s'interesse guère à la psychologie du prophète."[3]

---

[1] Karl Pichler, *Streit um das Christentum: Der Angriff des Kelsos und die Antwort des Origenes*, Regensburger Studien zur Theologie, Bd. 23 (Frankfurt am Main: Peter Lang, 1980), p. 1.

[2] For example, Völker, *Das Vollkommenheitsideal des Origenes*, Crouzel, *La "connaissance mystique"*, and Henri de Lubac, *Histoire et esprit: L'intelligence de l'Ecriture d'après Origène*, Théologie, no. 16 (Paris: Editions Montaigne, 1950).

[3] de Lubac, *Histoire et esprit*, p. 299.

If, in fact, he is not, Celsus forces the issue. Besides attacking one of the cornerstones of Christian apologetic, Celsus raises the question of spiritual power and effectiveness. Through the proclamations of the Logos in the prophets, the Christians had long claimed to possess insight into the workings of providence, and freedom from necessity and ignorance. Celsus asserts that this spiritual privilege is in reality the grossest form of spiritual deception, and one need only look at the character of the Christian prophets and their prophecies to see the work of the lower daemons. Origen's defense against this charge provides significant contributions to the understanding of religious debate in the ancient world, Christian views of inspiration, and Origen's own view of Scripture and the Christian life. It can be seen in an examination of Origen's response to specific charges, and his positive defense of the Old Testament prophets.

RESPONSE TO THE CHARGES

The occasional character of Origen's response to Celsus poses a significant obstacle to reconstructing major themes in *Against Celsus*. Origen tells us that his scheme, subsequent to *Cels*. 1.28, is simply to present the various charges of Celsus, and reply to them point by point. Henry Chadwick has shown that in doing so, Origen draws upon the ammunition supplied by generations of school polemic, and he thus often seems content with debater's points rather than substantive expositions.[4] Indeed, Karl Pichler has argued that Origen's primary concern is to discredit Celsus as an opponent by rhetorical means, rather than to provide a positive defense of Christianity.[5] In this respect, the easiest means of approach is to examine the response of Origen to specific charges made by Celsus. As we have seen, the charges dealing with prophecy include that of sorcery, delusion by phantasms, and obscurity. However, Origen's thought is not obscured by his method, and the issue of prophecy is substantive enough that he must deal with

---

[4]Henry Chadwick, "Origen, Celsus, and the Stoa," *Journal of Theological Studies* 48 (1947):34-49.

[5]Pichler, *Streit*, p. 298.

it extensively. Following an analysis of his reply to the charges, an examination of his positive defense of Christian reliance upon the prophets can be undertaken.

Sorcery. Celsus had asserted that rather than being inspired by divinity, the Hebrew prophets had instead been in collusion with earthly daemons. By depending upon the prophets, the Christians had been swindled by magicians and sorcerers. Celsus says about the Jews, and by extension, the Christians, "they shamelessly undertook to trace their genealogy back to the first offspring of sorcerers and deceivers, invoking the witness of vague and ambiguous utterances concealed in some dark obscurity" (*Cels.* 4.33). In reply, Origen adduces the power of the prophets over the magical system, their superior moral character, and their abstention from the daemons.

Origen responds to the charge of sorcery by showing the power of the prophets over the magical arts. He begins with a discourse on magic and a discussion of the power of names and magical formulas, intended, no doubt, to imply that Celsus is ignorant on the subject.[6] He affirms that magic is "a consistent system, which has principles known to a very few" (*Cels.* 1.24), and that names and incantations are used by experts to manipulate daemons. This system is a "natural" one; each daemon has a name which is natural to it, in the language of the country with which it is associated, and "when these names are pronounced in a particular sequence . . . they can be employed for certain purposes" (*Cels.* 1.24). By such skill, daemons can be bound to certain locations, (*Cels.* 3.34), invoked by spells, and oracles and healings can be obtained (*Cels.* 1.60).

So far Origen seems to be playing into Celsus' hands; if there is such a system of magic, based upon the knowledge of names and incantations, which vary by region because the daemons are associated with different countries, the Jews and Christians would seem simply to be using the name-magic of their own region when they invoke Moses, Abraham, Adonai, or Jesus. "Christians," Celsus says, "get the power

---

[6]Origen displays his erudition in citing Aristotle, the Stoics, and the Epicureans. See Chadwick, *Contra Celsum*, p. 23, n. 4-7, and Pichler, *Streit*, pp. 195-200.

which they seem to possess by pronouncing the names of certain daemons" (*Cels.* 1.6). Origen, however, responds by asserting that the Christians stand well above the realm of magic. The efficacy of the names of Abraham and Jesus does not indicate that such men are daemons; rather it indicates that they are more powerful than the daemons. Their power is a sign of their divine nature. Origen proclaims,

> To the Greeks I say this. Magi are in communion with daemons and by their formulas invoke them for the ends which they desire; and they succeed in these practices so long as nothing more divine and potent than the daemons and the spell that invokes them appears or is pronounced. But if anything more divine were to appear, the powers of the daemons would be destroyed.[7]

The names of Abraham, Isaac, and Jacob appear in magical formulas not because they are the names of daemons, but because of the mysterious divine power which these men had, which surpassed that to be found in the daemonic world (*Cels.* 4.34). The ancient prophets rose above the lower, corporeal sphere of the daemons, and the power of their names over the 'natural' system of magic is proof of this transcendence.

Origen's second line of defense in this debate revolves around the character of the doer, and the nature of the deed. He is willing to concede to Celsus that the doing of miracles or prophesying is not necessarily a proof of divinity. Celsus had asserted that the works of the Christians were simply magic tricks of wicked men. Origen agrees that wonders are ambiguous, and says,

> why should we not also examine carefully people who profess to do miracles, and see whether their lives and moral characters, and the results of their miracles, harm men or effect moral reformation? We should know in this way who serves daemons and causes such effects by means of certain spells and enchantments, and who has been on pure and holy ground

---

[7] *Cels.* 1.59.

before God in his own soul and spirit (and I think also in his body).[8]

Such an examination would vindicate Moses, who benefited an entire nation (*Cels.* 2.52), as well as Abraham and Jesus.

For Origen, the Christians and their prophets cannot have been deceived by the daemons because they abstain from any involvement with them. Indeed, the Jews effected this abstention from the daemons because of God's provision of prophets. While other nations were lured into intercourse with daemons by "the insatiable desire of man to know the future" (*Cels.* 1.36), the Jews, who were forbidden all divination or magic, were given the prophets. The prophets, says Origen, prophesied about affairs both mundane and divine in order to prevent the turning of their people to heathen divination and oracles. The Christians continue this abstention, and so remain well above the daemonic realm because of the virtue of their lives. Celsus had stated that the philosophical life, the life directed towards God, removed one from the realm and influence of the daemons. Origen responds by asserting that it is the Christian life, with its inherent virtue, morality, and devotion to God, that raises one above the daemonic world. He says,

> those who worship the supreme God through Jesus according to the way of Christianity, and live according to his gospel, and who use the appointed prayers continually and in the proper way day and night, are not caught either by magic or by daemons.[9]

Unlike the Greeks, says Origen, Christians have eschewed the daemonic realm, and the simple Christian, who lives virtuously and directs his life towards God, escapes its influence. The way of escape from the daemons is by having nothing to do with them, and the Christians, as well as the Jews, have accomplished this. "He who does no action loved by daemons," says Origen, "rises above bondage to all daemons and ascends above the portion of those said to be gods" (*Cels.* 8.5).

---

[8] *Cels.* 2.51.
[9] *Cels.* 6.41.

Origen's response to the charge of sorcery is that the Christians and their prophets are superior to the daemons who are manipulated by magical art. The names of the prophets have power over the daemonic world, because the prophets were inspired by God, rather than tricked by the daemons. More importantly, the lives and characters of the prophets testify to the nature of their message; they benefit mankind, and are themselves, by their virtue, beyond the influence of the wicked daemons. Origen's concern is thus to focus on the character of the prophets.

Phantoms and Terrors. As we have indicated, one of the characteristics which Celsus used in order to show that the prophets of the church were actually inspired by daemons, was the appearance of illusions and apparitions, or φάσματα, φαντάσματα and φαντασίαι. The Holy Spirit descending on Jesus at his baptism was a φάσμα (*Cels.* 1.43), and the appearance of Jesus after his resurrection was only a φαντασία (*Cels.* 2.60). Origen responds to this by arguing that dreams and visions are not necessarily signs of daemonic influence, and that the prophets saw non-corporeal realities with non-corporeal faculties.

Origen begins by questioning Celsus' negative estimate of illusions. He calls upon Plato for authority, and argues that Celsus' admission that people have visions of the dead simply confirms the fact that souls exist after death. Origen says the illusions which people see are in reality souls "subsisting in what is called the luminous body." "Thus," he says, "in his dialogue on the soul Plato says that 'shadowy apparitions' (σκιοειδῆ φαντάσματα) of men already dead have appeared to some people around tombs."[10]

More importantly, Origen questions Celsus' derogatory comments about φάσματα. Dreams are, after all, a highly respected method for learning about God and the future. Origen says,

> All who accept the doctrine of providence are obviously agreed
> in believing that in dreams many people form images in their
> minds (ὄναρ πεπίστευται πολλοὺς πεφαντασιῶσθαι),

---

[10]*Cels.* 2.60, *Phd.* 81 D.

some of divine things, others being announcements of future
events in life, whether clear or mysterious.[11]

Origen is appealing to contemporary views of dreams and prophecy.
Prophecy was often held to consist of images or representations
impressed upon the prophetic faculty of the soul, either by the soul
itself, or by some external inspiring force. As we have seen, there were
several factors which could affect the trustworthiness of such images,
but Origen argues that daytime occurrence should not immediately
disqualify them.[12] He concludes that it is not reprehensible that those
around Jesus at his baptism should have seen a φαντασίαν in the
daytime. Φαντασίαι are seen in the mind, are used by providence to
reveal the future, and are thus not necessarily a sign of daemonic
influence.

The point, however, which Origen makes is that seeing a φάσμα
or φαντασία is an actual seeing. A true reality may be perceived in a
φαντασία and is not necessarily manufactured; φάσμα need not be
πλάσμα (Cels. 3.3). In a dream or vision, an image is formed in the
mind; since in prophecy the realities which are perceived are divine, and
belong to the intelligible world, it is to be expected that they can be
seen only with the mind.[13] Even though the seeing is not done with
the eyes, it is a true seeing; indeed, for Origen, it is the most perfect
seeing. The prophets did in fact perceive φάσματα, but what they
saw was divine, and they saw them with a "divine sense."

The doctrine of the divine sense here plays a significant role in
Origen's refutation, and the importance of the apologetic context can be
seen in its development. While it appears in Origen's commentaries,

---

[11]Cels. 1.48.

[12]In so doing, he is going against common opinion, for daytime visions were
often held to be false. For example, Plutarch De gen. 589 D, "In popular belief,
on the other hand, it is only in sleep that men receive inspiration from on high;
and the notion that they are so influenced when awake and in full possession of
their faculties is accounted strange and incredible." See also Apuleius Met. 4.27.

[13]There is a similarity here between Origen's argument and that of the Simon
Magus of the Clementine literature, who claimed that the only secure truth was to
be found in mental images. See Hauck, " 'They Saw What They Said They Saw',"
pp. 239-243.

and in *On First Principles*,[14] its importance is apologetic, and as Rahner says, "Le polémique contre l'Ἀληθὴς Λόγος de Celse décida Origène à développer sa doctrine."[15] It plays two important roles in the apologetic situation. One of these is to refute Celsus' charge concerning the corporeality of Christian doctrine, and in this setting the notion of the divine sense plays the same role as Origen's allegorical defense of Scripture. Celsus claims, says Origen, that "we believe we shall see God with eyes of the body and hear his voice with our ears and touch him with our sensible hands." To this Origen replies that Celsus, materially oriented as he is, fails to understand that when Scripture talks of seeing, hearing, or touching God, "there are some hands which are given that name with an allegorical meaning." What Scripture is referring to is a "superior and incorporeal sense" (τῆς κρείττονος αἰσθήσεως καὶ οὐ σωματικῆς), a spiritual sense analogous to the bodily senses (*Cels*. 7.34).

In this respect, Scripture would seem to be speaking merely figuratively or metaphorically.[16] However, in replying to Celsus' charge of φάσμα, the second context in which this concept is important, Origen uses it in a much more serious fashion. The prophets, while they may have seen φάσματα, really perceived; they perceived an incorporeal truth, with an incorporeal faculty. Certainly, says Origen, when Scripture says God spoke, or the heavens were opened and a dove descended, we are not to think that the air was vibrated, or that the sky was physically split. Rather, a divine truth was communicated incorporeally, and perceived with incorporeal senses, which are analogous to the physical senses. There is a sight which sees τὰ κρείττονα σωμάτων, hearing which hears sounds οὐχὶ ἐν

---

[14]Origen's foundation for this is a variant reading of Proverbs 2:5:, ὅτι αἴσθησιν θείαν εὑρήσεις. This is a variant for the Septuagint's καὶ ἐπίγνωσιν θεοῦ εὑρήσεις. The variant reading also occurs in Clement *Strom.* 1.4. See Karl Rahner, "Le début d'une doctrine des cinq sens spirituels chez Origène," *Revue d'ascetique et de mystique* 13 (1932):113-145, and Marguerite Harl, "La 'bouche' et le 'coeur' de l'apôtre: deux images bibliques du 'sens divin' de l'homme (Proverbes 2,5) chez Origène," in *Forma Futuri: Studi in onore del Cardinale Michele Pellegrino* (Torino: Bottega d'Erasmo, 1975), pp. 17-42.

[15]Rahner, "Debut," p. 117.

[16]So Rahner, "Debut," p. 124.

ἀέρι τὴν οὐσίαν ἐχουσῶν, and so on (*Cels*. 1.48). The point in this context is that, "In this way [the prophets] saw what they record that they saw, and they heard what they say they heard" (*Cels*. 1.48). More importantly, however, this argument refutes the charge of daemonic involvement associated with the production of φάσματα. The divine senses are possessed only by those who are themselves divine. Origen says, "Anyone who looks into this subject more deeply will say that there is, as the scripture calls it, a certain generic divine sense which only the man who is blessed finds on this earth" (*Cels*. 1.48). This sense is given by God only to those who have made themselves worthy, and have lifted themselves above the realm of the material.[17] The prophets were so blessed, and with a divine sense "they touched the Word by faith so that an emanation came from him to them which healed them" (*Cels*. 1.48). Origen again emphasizes the character of the prophets and the nature of their prophetic experience in order to refute the charges of sorcery which Celsus has made. In his positive defense of Christian reliance upon prophecy he will examine what sort of men the prophets are, and what sort of experience they had.

Obscurity. Another of the manifestations of the daemons and their deception of the Christians, for Celsus, was the obscure and ambiguous nature of Jewish and Christian prophecies. According to Celsus, Moses' writings were "vague and ambiguous utterances concealed in some dark obscurity" (*Cels*. 4.33), and contemporary Christian prophets produced "incomprehensible, incoherent, and utterly obscure utterances," which were useful only for sorcery (*Cels*. 7.9). Origen responds by asserting that the prophecies are clear on the moral level, and while they have deeper meaning which is difficult to understand, the prophets themselves had clear insight and understood this meaning.

Origen says, "The prophets, according to the will of God, said without any obscurity whatever could be at once understood as beneficial to their hearers and helpful towards attaining moral reformation" (*Cels*. 7.10). Unlike the Greek writings, which are

---

[17]Origen says the divine sense is "not of the eyes but of a pure heart" (*Prin*. 1.1.9). According to Harl, it is "fonctionnement supérieur du coeur pur, c'est-à-dire de l'intellect non pas seulement purifié mais divinement inspiré, illuminé." "La bouche et la coeur," p. 33, n. 21.

impious and harmful in their literal meaning, the Christian writings are perfectly clear and beneficial even to the most incapable of readers. In their own day, the prophets were understood at the literal level, and "as a result of what the prophets proclaimed, cities were set on the right path, men were restored to health, famines ceased, and furthermore, it is clear that the whole Jewish nation came to form a colony when they left Egypt and came to Palestine in accordance with the oracles" (*Cels.* 8.46).

The prophecies also have a deeper meaning, which Celsus has failed to grasp. However, this deeper meaning was not hidden in the oracles of the prophets without their knowledge, but rather, the prophets had a clear understanding of their message, and intentionally concealed the deeper truths. The prophets were inspired by the Holy Spirit, and rather than losing consciousness of what they were saying,[18] actually received a clearer insight into divine reality. Origen says, "Because of the touch, so to speak, of what is called the Holy Spirit on their soul they possessed a clear mental vision (διορατικώτεροί τε τὸν νοῦν ἐγίνοντο, *Cels.* 7.4)." The concealment of their deeper doctrines occurred not because they were ignorant of them, but with their full knowledge, for the benefit of their hearers. According to Origen, Moses composed the Pentateuch in full possession of his faculties, according to a well-conceived plan, and according to the rules of rhetoric. He says, "But in his five books Moses acted like a distinguished orator who pays attention to outward form and everywhere keeps the carefully concealed meaning of his words" (*Cels.* 1.18). The Christian writings were not obscure to those who wrote them, and are ambiguous only to those of limited capacity. Origen's concern, in this reply to a specific charge of Celsus, is once again to consider the character of the prophet, and the nature of his experience.

In Origen's response to each of these charges, the common factor is his reliance upon the character of the prophet, and the nature of the prophetic experience. While his replies often consist of debater's points and an overriding desire to belittle his opponent, Origen is concerned to

---

[18] *Cels.* 7.3. This is in contrast to the Pythia who is led "into a state of ecstasy and frenzy so that she loses possession of her consciousness (ὡς μηδαμῶς αὐτὴν ἑαυτῇ παρακολουθεῖν)."

focus on the question of what sort of people the prophets were. The question, as Celsus raised it, is whether the prophets were entrapped by daemons in the lower order of the material world, or whether they succeeded in lifting themselves beyond it. Origen argues that they had, and that an examination of their lives and intellectual abilities and experience proves as much.

DEFENSE OF THE PROPHETS

> But Moses was not a sorcerer but a pious man, dedicated to the
> God of the universe; and partaking of a divine spirit, he gave
> laws to the Hebrews as God prompted him, and recorded events
> as they actually happened.[19]

Origen's response to the charges made by Celsus concerning the Christian reliance on prophecy, while often aimed more at showing Celsus' polemical incompetence than at a substantive defense, focuses upon the lives and experience of the prophets. For Origen, the issue is whether the prophets were in communion with God or the daemons. The question is thus one of spiritual discernment and spiritual combat. As Origen carries out his positive defense of the prophets, this concern leads him to focus on the dangers of prophecy, in the context of spiritual combat, the character of the prophets' lives and minds, and the character of their prophetic experience. He uses his understanding of the spiritual life to show that the prophets ascended above the realm of the daemons.

The Dangers of Prophecy. For Origen, as for Celsus, prophecy and divination are closely tied to the knowledge of God, and thus provide a central battleground for spiritual and daemonic conflict. According to Origen, powers of divination and knowledge of the future are not proof

---

[19]*Cels.* 3.5.

of divine influence; in and of themselves, they are *adiaphora*.[20]
However, human beings have, says Origen, "an insatiable desire to
know the future," and the daemons exploit this desire in order to deceive
the human race (*Cels*. 1.36). One of the reasons that God gave
prophets to the Israelites was to keep them out of the dangerous realm
of divination, and this is why, says Origen, apparently in response to a
sneer by Celsus, the Jewish prophets prophesied about things so
mundane as the lost asses of Saul. If the prophets hadn't supplied such
information, the Jews would have turned, against God's command, to
oracles who would.[21]

To follow this "insatiable desire" into the realm of oracles,
divination, and indiscriminate prophecy is to enter a dangerous sphere of
spiritual influence. Origen, like Celsus, feels that knowledge of the
future is the province of daemons. However, unlike Celsus, Origen
views this province in an unequivocally negative manner. Celsus had
argued that the daemons were the ἐπόπτοι, the bureaucrats of
providence who dispensed the benefits, including foreknowledge,
necessary for a comfortable life on earth (*Cels*. 8.33). Origen allows
the daemons a place in the providential bureaucracy, but argues that it is
the angels who are the overseers, while the daemons are the
executioners, who are permitted by God to deal out the pain,
punishment, and tragedy necessary within the scheme of providence.[22]
Against Celsus, who says that the daemons are morally neutral, Origen
asserts that "the name of daemons is always applied to evil powers
without the grosser body" (*Cels*. 5.5).

---

[20]*Cels*. 3.25, 4.96, 7.5.   However, Origen says in *Cels*. 6.10, "The
proclamation of future events is the mark of divinity, since they are not foretold
by a natural human faculty."

[21]*Cels*. 1.36. Cf. 1 Sam 9.

[22]*Cels*. 8.31.   The daemons receive power from God to cause famines,
droughts, and plagues. The purpose of these catastrophes is the conversion of
human beings, the training of the human race, and the revelation of the true
characters of both good and wicked people. These external events are not truly
evil, because virtue and vice are within the soul. Physical evil plays an
educational role in the providential care of humanity. See *Cels*. 6.55-56, and Hal
Koch, *Pronoia und Paideusis*, pp. 152-159.

Origen agrees with Celsus that the daemons are souls that have fallen from their heavenly home. However, he disagrees in placing them below humanity on the scale of departure from God. According to Origen, the daemons sinned the "deepest" at the original rebellion, and thus have been cast down to earth without the corrective benefit of being bound to a body.[23] Origen speaks of the human soul as midway between the fate of the angels and that of the daemons, and says that after death,

> the pure soul, which is not weighed down by the leaden weights of evil, is carried on high to the regions of the purer and ethereal bodies . . . whereas the bad soul, that is dragged down to earth by its sins and has not even the power to make a recovery, is carried here and roams about, in some cases at tombs where also apparitions of shadowy souls have been seen, in other cases simply round about the earth.[24]

Although the daemons are very low on the scale of wickedness, they do not possess the "grosser body,"[25] and thus have the power of foreknowledge.[26] This power is exercised at the oracle sites, where they have been bound by those who know the appropriate spells (*Cels.* 3.34), and also in traditional forms of divination, which usually utilize animals to give omens. According to Origen, the daemons have a kinship with certain animals, and move them to give signs. He says, "They creep into the most rapacious wild beasts and other very wicked animals and impel them to do what they want . . . or turn the images in the minds of such animals towards flights and movements of a particular sort" (*Cels.* 4.92). Moses knew about this relationship of the

---

[23]"But there remained some souls who had not sinned so greatly as to become daemons, nor on the other hand so very lightly as to become angels. God therefore made the present world and bound the soul to the body as a punishment" (*Prin.* 1.8.1).

[24]*Cels.* 7.5.

[25]*Cels.* 5.5, τοῦ παχυτέρου σώματος.

[26]*Cels.* 4.92, "They have some perception of the future, in that they are unclothed by earthly bodies." See Henri Crouzel, "L'anthropologie d'Origène dans la perspective du combat spirituel," *Revue d'ascetique et de mystique* 31 (1955), p. 381.

daemons and animals, and thus gave the laws concerning unclean animals to protect the Jews from daemonic influence (*Cels.* 4.93).

The danger implicit in the daemonic nature of divination and false prophecy derives from the fact that the daemons are hostile to humanity. "They use their power to know the future," Origen says, "which is morally neither good nor bad, to deceive men and distract them from God and pure piety towards Him" (*Cels.* 7.5). In much the same manner as Celsus, Origen asserts that the daemons' goal is to restrain humanity down within their earthly sphere, and prevent the mind of human beings from reaching up to God. They accomplish this by ensnaring the mind in the love of material things, by deceiving the mind with false images, and by destroying the very rationality of the mind itself.

The daemons ensnare the mind in materiality by using objects and omens to predict the future. The function of animals, material objects, and physical signs in the process of divination is, according to Origen, simply to turn the mind from the invisible God to the visible world. The involvement with the visible world in this way entraps the mind at that level. Origen says, "Their desire is that men may be caught by the prophetic power in the irrational animals and not seek God who contains the whole world but may fall in their reasoning to the level of earth and the birds and serpents" (*Cels.* 4.92).

However, the daemons also entrap humanity by insinuating false images and deceptions within the mind itself. This had been the argument of Celsus against the Christians; unknowingly, their prophets, who consorted with daemons, had been deceived by false images produced in the mind by daemons. We have seen that Origen responded to this charge by asserting that the prophets perceived their truths, not under daemonic influence, but with a divine sense, and we will see in his discussion of prophecy how one avoids this influence. He is, however, aware of this danger. "We do not want any daemon," he says, "to get a place in our mind (τὸ ἡγεμονικόν) or any hostile spirit to turn our imagination (τὸ φανταστικόν) where he wills."[27] In *On First Principles* Origen tells us that external forces are able to

---

[27]*Cels.* 4.95. Angels can also produce images in the mind: εἴτ ἀγγέλου εἴθ' οὑτινοσοῦν φαντασιοῦντος τὴν ψυχήν, *Cels.* 1.66.

produce impressions in the imagination, and quite often these forces are the hostile daemons, seeking to turn humanity away from God.[28]

More significantly, however, the function of the daemons is to destroy rationality itself. Origen feels that Celsus himself is a good example of the irrational activity of the daemons. He says of Celsus, "Sometimes his mind is distracted by the daemons, and sometimes, when he recovers his senses a little from the irrationality which the daemons produce, he gets a glimpse of the truth" (*Cels.* 8.63). According to Origen, the daemons have produced "ecstasies" in the rational faculty (λογισμός) of Celsus, by which, says Origen, he is "for the most part overcome."[29]

Ecstasy, a product of the daemons, also plays an important role in Origen's discussion of prophecy. The hellenistic tradition regarded ecstasy and prophetic frenzy as a respectable product of the prophetic experience, and Lucian's description of how Alexander the false prophet aroused reverence by chewing soapwort and foaming at the mouth is evidence of the power of this viewpoint (Lucian *Alex.* 12). Thinkers such as Philo affirmed prophetic ecstasy and argued that in the highest point of the ascent of the prophet's soul, the mind of the prophet is no longer "in itself," and has ceased to carry out its illuminating and governing function (Philo *Rer. div. her.* 264).

Origen, who agrees with much of Philo's characterization of the prophets, parts company with him on the issue of ecstasy. Ecstasy was particularly suspect in Origen's day because of the excesses of Montanism. At issue in the Montanist crisis was the question of παρακολουθέω; whether the mind of the prophet was present and attentive during the prophetic experience.[30] The Montanists argued that possession and prophetic frenzy were the mark of the true prophet,[31] while the orthodox asserted that such frenzy was foreign to

---

[28]*Prin.* 3.1.3, 3.2.2.

[29]*Cels.* 8.63. Chadwick translates ἐκστάσεις as "distractions." *Contra Celsum*, p. 500.

[30]See Epiphanius *Haer.* 48.3.

[31]So Tertullian *Adv. Marc.* 4.12, "the principle which we maintain in the New Prophecy, that to grace ecstasy or rapture is incident. For when a man is rapt in the Spirit, especially when he beholds the glory of God, or when God speaks through him, he necessarily loses his sensation, because he is overshadowed with

the experience of the church, and that the mind of the prophet must pay attention to, and benefit from, his inspiration.[32] Origen's concern is for the rationality of the prophet, and the increase of his mental faculties. He rejects the position of Philo, and, using language similar to that employed in the debate over Montanism, asserts that divine inspiration does not lead to ecstasy, and any prophetic experience which produces a decrease of rationality is from the daemons. He says,

> Furthermore, it is not the work of a divine spirit to lead the alleged prophetess into a state of ecstasy and frenzy so that she loses possession of her consciousness. The person inspired by the divine spirit ought to have derived from it far more benefit than anyone . . . he ought to possess the clearest vision at the very time when the deity is in communion with him.[33]

Involvement with false prophecy, and involvement with the daemons thus leads to a loss of rationality and free will. It is daemonic rather than divine inspiration which injures the mind, and in the case of the Pythia, who loses consciousness under inspiration, Origen asks, "what sort of spirit must we think it which poured darkness upon her mind and rational thinking? Its character must be that of the race of daemons" (*Cels.* 7.4). In the spiritual combat in the human soul at risk is reason, freedom, and the ability to clearly perceive the spiritual realities.

True Prophecy. For Origen, the prophets are the champions in this spiritual conflict. In his defense of the Hebrew prophets, he asserts that Celsus' charges of sorcery and daemon-involvement are unfounded because the prophets are the best examples of those who have overcome the daemons and the irrationality they produce. The prophets stand at the summit of the spiritual path, and their achievement is characterized, for Origen, by the life of virtue and the attainment of true rationality. The defense of the prophets can thus best be seen by an examination of

---

the power of God, -- a point concerning which there is a question between us and the carnally-minded."

[32]See Eusebius *Hist. Eccl.* 5.16-19 and Epiphanius *Haer.* 48.

[33]*Cels.* 7.3.

Origen's treatment in *Against Celsus* of the intellectual and spiritual life.

As many scholars have noted, one of the chief areas of disagreement between Origen and Celsus concerns the need for special revelation.[34] Origen contests the ability of the soul to make its own way to the knowledge of God, and asserts instead that the soul is in a spiritual struggle from which it cannot extricate itself without help.[35] He is willing to grant that there is a 'common revelation' which is available to humanity. This consists of a kinship with God, that is, a participation in the logos, common to all rational creatures (*Cels.* 3.40). The human soul, in particular, is made in the image of the logos.[36] Origen says,

> But when [one] looks at the rational beings (τοῖς λογικοῖς), he will see reason (λόγον) which is common to men and to divine and heavenly beings, and probably also to the supreme God Himself. This explains why he is said to have been made in the image of God; for the image of the supreme God is his reason (Logos).[37]

This common revelation is sufficient only for a potential for virtue and a knowledge of general moral principles (*Cels.* 4.26). In response to Celsus' charge that Christianity's ethics are rather commonplace, Origen says,

> I have to reply to this that for people who affirm the righteous judgment of God, it would have been impossible to believe in the penalty inflicted for sins unless in accordance with the universal ideas all men had a sound conception of moral principles. There is therefore nothing amazing about it if the

---

[34] For example, Henri Crouzel, *La "connaissance mystique*," p. 127.

[35] See Crouzel, "L'anthropologie."

[36] For a treatment of this aspect of Origen's anthropology see Henri Crouzel, *Théologie de l'image de Dieu chez Origène* (Aubier: Editions Montaigne, 1956), pp. 168-171.

[37] *Cels.* 4.85.

same God has implanted in the soul of men the truths which He taught through the prophets and the Saviour.[38]

This knowledge, according to Origen, who here refers to Paul, is only adequate to render all people without excuse (*Cels.* 1.4). Origen says that Celsus has not taken seriously Plato's statement, "Now to find the Maker and Father of this universe is difficult, and after finding him it is impossible to declare him to all men" (*Cels.* 7.42). Indeed, not only is it difficult for unaided human nature to find God, it is impossible, and Origen says, "we affirm that human nature is not sufficient in any way to seek for God and to find Him in His pure nature, unless it is helped by the God who is object of the search" (*Cels* 7.42). The philosophers have, with great effort and after a long time, achieved a limited amount of truth, but in general have shown great presumption in making statements, "about immense subjects as though they had understood them, and because they seriously maintain that they have perceived the truth about problems when they cannot be understood without superior inspiration and divine power" (*Cels.* 4.30). The inability of the soul to know God is a result of the impurity of the fallen soul, and its consequent limited capacity for the divine. Origen says that this limitation is "partly because of the defilement of the mind that is bound to a human 'body of humiliation', partly because of its restricted capacity to comprehend God" (*Cels.* 6.17).

Origen speaks of what is required for knowledge of God in varying ways. He often calls it simply "divine grace" (*Cels.* 7.44), or "superior inspiration,"[39] and it includes the indwelling of, or participation in, the Holy Spirit. In the apologetic context of *Against Celsus*, Origen often speaks of inspiration taking place by a "certain divine spirit" (*Cels.* 3.3). This is the Holy Spirit, who is given "only to those in whom [God] judges it right to dwell."[40] This judgement is based upon

---

[38]*Cels.* 1.4. These are the κοιναὶ ἐννοίαι of Stoicism; see Chadwick, *Contra Celsum*, p. 8, n. 6.

[39]*Cels.* 4.30, ἐπιπνοίας κρείττονος καὶ θειοτέρας δυνάμεως.

[40]*Cels.* 5.1. Origen does speak of a communication of God's spirit to all mankind (*Cels.* 4.38, and *Prin.* 1.3.3). However, he seems to be distinguishing between a general participation of rational creatures in God, and a special gift of the Spirit to the worthy. He says in *Prin.* 1.3.7, "Thus, therefore, the working of

capacity. Origen says, "God is always giving a share of His own Spirit to those who are able to partake of Him, though He dwells in those who are worthy not by being cut into sections and divided up" (*Cels.* 6.70).

This grace also consists of the work of the Logos in the mind. For Origen, as for Celsus, the path to knowledge of God consists of raising the eyes of the soul from the things of sense to the intelligible world. In reply to Celsus' discourse on Being and Becoming, and his description of the Platonic methods for the knowledge of God, Origen says that Paul speaks of something similar when he says, "We look not to the things that are seen but the things that are unseen."[41] Origen says,

> It is in this way also that the disciples of Jesus look at the things that are becoming, so that they use them as steps to the contemplation of the nature of intelligible things. "For the invisible things of God," that is the intelligible things, "are understood by the things that are made" and "from the creation of the world are clearly seen" by the process of thought. And when they have ascended from the created things . . . to the invisible things of God they do not stop there . . . they ascend to the eternal power of God, and in a word, to His Divinity.[42]

The ascent to God is the ascent of the mind from the sensible to the intelligible realities, and this is undertaken, as Origen says, "by the process of thought (ἐν τῷ νοεῖσθαι)." This is the work of the Logos, the source of all reason (*Cels.* 7.46). Origen also describes it as illumination (*Cels.* 6.17), and as an opening of the eyes of the soul, "to which the Logos gives the power of sight."[43]   The Logos, says Origen, "changed our thoughts from considering all objects of sense

---

the power of God the Father and God the Son is spread indiscriminately over all created beings, but a share in the Holy Spirit is possessed, we find, by the saints alone."

[41] 2 Cor. 4:18; *Cels.* 7.46.

[42] *Cels.* 7.46.

[43] *Cels.* 7.39. Völker describes the *Aufstieg* of the soul, and notes that visions form the initial stages, and are replaced by illumination. *Vollkommenheitsideal*, p. 71.

... and ... led us to honour the supreme God with upright conduct and prayers" (*Cels.* 3.34).

According to Origen, all rational creatures share in the Logos, and by that participation possess a potential for the knowledge of God and virtue. However, the illuminating activity of God, this "superior inspiration" which is necessary to awaken the eyes of the soul, is, says Origen, given only according to capacity and merit. The Logos relates to each individual only according to his ability to perceive the deeper realities. Thus at Jesus' baptism "the man who has become hard of hearing in his soul does not perceive that God is speaking" (*Cels.* 2.72). At the transfiguration the Logos appeared in different forms to those who were watching, according to the capacity of each to perceive. "To those who are still down below and are not prepared to ascend," says Origen, "the Logos 'has not form nor beauty' " (*Cels.* 6.77).

For Origen, the capacity or ability to receive the gift of the knowledge of God is governed by progress in virtue, or merit. Indeed, virtue itself is the progressive capacity to perceive divine reality, because it consists in turning away from the lower world of sense, and towards the intelligible world.[44] Origen says,

> The words "Depart from evil and do good" refer neither to physical good or evil things as they are called by some, nor to external things, but to the good and evil of the soul. He who has departed from what is evil in this sense and who has done good actions of this kind, as desiring to see the true life, will come to possess it.[45]

'Bad' souls are those who turn away from the intelligible world to the world of sense, and they are "dragged down to earth by their sins, and [have] not even power to make a recovery" (*Cels.* 7.5). Good souls are those who are seeking to know God, and are turning towards the eternal realities. Origen says, "It is not right for a heart that has been defiled to look upon God; that which can deservedly perceive Him who is pure must be pure also" (*Cels.* 6.69).

---

[44]See Crouzel, *La "connaissance mystique,"* pp. 443-495.
[45]*Cels.* 6.54.

It is according to this progress in opening the eye of the soul that the divine grace of illumination is given. According to Origen, the veil which covers the heart "is taken away by God's gift when He perceives a man who has done everything in his own power, and by use has exercised his sense to distinguish good and evil" (*Cels.* 4.50). Origen says that the knowledge of God, unavailable to unaided human nature, is given to those "who by God's foreknowledge have been previously determined, because they would live lives worthy of Him after He was made known to them" (*Cels.* 7.44). The Holy Spirit dwells in those "who are able to partake of Him. . . . He dwells in those who are worthy" (*Cels.* 6.70), and it is the nature of the Logos, says Origen, "to nourish the human soul, in accordance with the merits of each individual." According to Origen, the Logos has an absolute knowledge of God, because he possesses absolute merit. All others are able to participate in the Logos, in accordance with their merit,[46] and, says Origen, "Only those who are truly wise and genuinely pious are nearer to communion with God" (*Cels.* 4.96).

The increase in capacity and merit, and thus knowledge of God, is carried out by free will. When Celsus criticizes the Christian God for his inability to win over the human race, Origen responds that it is certainly within God's abilities to convert by divine power, but that this would destroy free will, and "if you take away the element of free will from virtue, you also destroy its essence" (*Cels.* 6.57). Divine illumination comes as a result of the choice of the free will to turn to God, and indeed, preserves and increases that freedom. Souls stand between the upper and the lower world, between good and evil, free to either raise the eyes of the soul, or to lower them.[47]

---

[46]*Cels.* 6.17. Here Origen's Christology plays a role in his discussion of merit, and thus in his apologetic. Christ's human soul was intimately joined to the Logos because of its unique merit. The prophets have a similar, but lesser, experience. He says, "a derived knowledge is possessed by those whose minds are illuminated by the divine Logos himself, absolute understanding and knowledge of the Father is possessed by himself alone in accordance with his merits."

[47]For a recent discussion of the place of the soul in Origen's anthropology, see Marie-Joseph Pierre, "L'âme dans l'anthropologie d'Origène," *Proche-Orient Chrétien* 34 (1984):21-65.

For Origen, the history of humanity has therefore been one of continual persuasion by God, in which God by the Logos has been working to return the soul to himself.[48] Origen says, "He has always cared for the reformation of the rational being and given opportunities of virtue" (*Cels.* 4.7). When Celsus questions the tardy appearance of the savior, Origen responds that throughout history God has actively been recalling human beings, and says, "In fact, nothing has been or will be neglected by God, who at each season makes what He should be making in a world of alteration and change" (*Cels.* 4.69).

This persuasion effort on the part of God has been carried out in several ways. First, by his providence, God has so arranged the world as to challenge humanity's intellectual abilities. In the first periods of the human race, more help was granted in order to allow infantile humanity to survive and pursue the life of virtue (*Cels.* 4.80). In later stages people were more needy, as they were required to exercise their intellect to obtain necessities of life and protection from the wild animals, "so that for these reasons one might admire the providence which made the rational creature for his benefit more needy than the irrational animals" (*Cels.* 4.76). Besides the providential ordering of the world, God also has been continually sending prophets to turn humanity to the life of virtue. "In each generation," says Origen, "His Word descends into holy souls and makes them friends of God and prophets" (*Cels.* 4.3). Some generations have exceeded others in prophetic activity, according to need, but God has continually been persuading humanity through the prophets to turn to him. Origen says, "God . . . willed to tell men about these things [good and evil] through the prophets, in order that those who understood their words might be made lovers of what is better, and be on their guard against the opposite" (*Cels.* 6.45). God has also, however, been directly aiding human beings with divine power, or the Holy Spirit. In the early stages of humanity, and even in the present, this type of help or persuasion takes the form of dreams, visions, and visitations by angels who "regard as kinsmen and friends those who imitate their piety towards God, and assist those who call upon God."[49] However, this

---

[48]Koch, *Pronoia und Paideusis*, p. 18.

[49]*Cels.* 8.34; see *Cels.* 4.80.

type of aid also includes the gift of divine power and indwelling of the Holy Spirit. "God is always," says Origen, "giving a share of His own Spirit to those who are able to partake of Him" (*Cels*. 6.70). He always wants to make himself known, and "either dwells in certain people Himself by a mysterious divine power, or sends His Christ" (*Cels*. 4.6). The incarnation of the Logos is simply the latest and best example of God's continual persuasion of humanity.

However, as we have seen above, the daemons have carried out a parallel program of persuasion. Ever since the beginning they have attempted to prevent the turning of humanity to God. Their goal has been to use their powers of divination and magic to hold the human race down in the material world, to bind humanity to the love of the sensible world, and to prevent the ascent of the soul to God. Origen says, "Their desire is that men may be caught by the prophetic power in the irrational animals and not seek God" (*Cels*. 4.92). Their efforts have been "to hinder the soul's ascent and journey by means of virtue and a restoration of true piety towards God" (*Cels*. 7.3).

Thus for Origen, the human condition is in a state of spiritual warfare. In *On First Principles* he clearly indicates that the human soul on earth stands between the influence of logos, the spirit, and the divine on one hand, and the restraining power of the daemons on the other (*Prin*. 3.2.2). As Henri Crouzel has argued, this concept of spiritual combat is one of the motivating forces behind Origen's anthropology, and Crouzel views the elevation of the soul above the daemons' influence, towards God, as a central concern of Origen's thought.[50] For Origen, this combat is carried out by the choice of the free will, and one must decide which influence will govern the direction of one's mind. Origen says that, just as a man who gets his hair cut must offer himself to the barber, so the one who is persuaded by God must offer himself, by his own will, to that persuasion.[51] Conversely, one can also offer himself to the persuasion of daemons, and by love of their activity, allow them a place in the mind. Origen says in *On First Principles*,

---

[50]Crouzel, "L'anthropologie," p. 365.

[51]*Cels*. 6.57. This is a common image used by grammarians to illustrate the middle voice. Chadwick, *Contra Celsum*, p. 373, n. 3.

Just as holy and stainless souls, when they have devoted
themselves to God . . . acquire thereby a communion with the
divine nature and win the grace of prophecy and of the other
divine gifts, so too, must we think that those who show
themselves fit subjects for the opposing powers, that is, those
who adopt a work and manner of life and purpose agreeable to
them, receive their inspiration and become participators in their
wisdom and doctrine. The result of this is that they are filled
with the operations of those spirits to whose service they have
once subjected themselves.[52]

This understanding of the spiritual life forms the undergirding for
Origen's defense of the Old Testament prophets, and plays a major role
in the apologetic context. For Origen, once one understands the nature
of the spiritual warfare and the life of virtue, it is evident that the
prophets experienced true inspiration and communion with God, while
hellenistic forms of prophecy remain in the realm of the daemons.
According to Origen, "Only those who are truly wise and genuinely
pious are nearer to God. Such is the character of our prophets and of
Moses" (*Cels.* 4.96). The proof of the prophets is founded on the
purity of their lives and their wisdom, or heightened rationality.

Pious and Inspired Men. In response to Celsus' charge of sorcery,
Origen replies that Moses was not a γόης, but a εὐσεβής ἀνήρ.
Origen's defense of the prophets, and his claim that true prophecy is to
be found in the Christian camp, revolves around his claims concerning
the character and experience of the Old Testament prophets. He claims
that they were of a pure and pious character, and that their experience
was one of true divine inspiration.

Origen describes the character of the prophets as that of utmost purity
and piety. They were chosen by providence, he says, "on account of the
quality of their lives, which was of unexampled courage and freedom"
(*Cels.* 7.7). He speaks of their "more active and zealous life" (*Cels.*
4.8), and calls them "truly wise and pious" (*Cels.* 4.96). Their outward
lives, however, are only of passing interest; he is more interested in

---

[52]*Prin.* 3.3.3.

describing their souls. The souls of the prophets are sacred, pure, holy and pious. The prophet is able to prophesy because he "has been on pure and holy ground before God in his own soul and spirit" (*Cels.* 2.51). Far from being in contact with earthly daemons, the prophet has so purified his soul that it is worthy of divine inspiration.

The experience of the prophet, therefore, reflects this purity of soul. According to Origen, the prophets were inspired (θεοφορέω, *Cels.* 4.95), illuminated in mind and soul (*Cels.* 7.7, 7.21), participated in, and were filled with, divinity and a divine spirit (*Cels.* 3.5, 3.81, 4.8, 7.4). According to Origen, Moses and the prophets were lifted above the sensible realm, and even above the realm of the daemons, and attained communion with God. He says,

> we are free to believe that in the pure and pious soul of Moses, who rose above all that is created, and united himself to the Creator of the universe, there dwelt a divine spirit which showed the truth about God far clearer than Plato.[53]

In all of this language, Origen is asserting, against Celsus' claim, that the prophets were well beyond the influence of the daemons, were themselves divine in soul and mind, and spoke by divine inspiration. The significance of these claims can be seen in the context of Origen's views on the nature and dangers of false prophecy, and the way to true knowledge of God and true prophecy: for Origen, the prophets stand at the summit of the spiritual life and the life of virtue. The candidates for the receipt of the Holy Spirit and divine inspiration must be those who have purified themselves with the life of virtue. Origen says, "And that which sees God is a pure heart, from which evil thoughts no longer proceed" (*Cels.* 7.33). In refuting Celsus' reliance on traditional means of divination Origen argues, "For the knowledge of the future the true God uses neither irrational animals nor ordinary men, but the most sacred and holy human souls whom he inspires and makes prophets" (*Cels.* 4.95). Unlike Apollo, who seems to prefer to ravish women (*Cels.* 3.25), the Holy Spirit only dwells in pure souls of men. The

---

[53]*Cels.* 1.19. This language is similar to that of Philo. See Philo *Som.* 2.229, *Vit. Mos.* 1.27.

Old Testament prophets, therefore, are those who have distinguished themselves by their virtue, and who were chosen because of the superior character of their lives. Origen asserts,

> They were chosen by providence to be entrusted with the divine spirit and with the utterances He inspired on account of the quality of their lives, which was of unexampled courage and freedom. ... They always looked upon God and the invisible things which are not seen with the eyes of the senses.[54]

The prophets of Scripture were the spiritual athletes of their generation.[55] In each age the Holy Spirit chooses the best candidates, and Origen says, "It is not surprising that there have been prophets in certain generations, who on account of their more active and zealous life surpassed other prophets in their reception of divine inspiration" (*Cels.* 4.8). Rather than being charlatans deceived by the daemons, as Celsus said, the prophets were the spiritual champions of their day, and their inspiration is guaranteed by the character of their lives.

Because of the quality of their lives, and their consequent inspiration, the prophets were not only pure, but wise. As those who were successfully on the path up towards God, the prophets, according to Origen, had intimate communion with God, and perceived deep spiritual realities. Says Origen, "some were wise before they received the gift of prophecy and divine inspiration, while others became wise before they had been illuminated in mind by the actual gift of prophecy itself" (*Cels.* 7.7). Paul, who falls into this category, was "illuminated in his soul" (*Cels.* 7.21), and perceived the distinction between sensible and intelligible things (*Cels.* 3.48), while Ezekiel perceived the way in which the soul enters the divine realm (*Cels.* 6.23). Moses, the best example of true inspiration, rose in soul, "above all that is created, and united himself to the Creator of the universe" (*Cels.* 1.19).

---

[54]*Cels.* 7.7. Cf. Plutarch *De gen.* 593 B, "so too our betters (the daemons) take the best of us, as from a herd, and setting a mark on us, honour us with a peculiar and exceptional schooling."

[55]In the *Against Celsus*, however, Origen does not use the term ἀθλητής for the prophets, but rather Celsus' terminology of σόφος and ἔνθεος. See Völker, *Vollkommenheitsideal*, pp.187-189.

For Origen, particularly within the apologetic context, this kind of spiritual insight and communion with God consists of a heightened ability to perceive spiritual reality, and a heightened rationality. Concerning perception, Origen expands upon the Platonic 'eye of the soul' terminology to say that the prophets had a 'divine sense.' We have seen that in his reply to Celsus' charge of φάσμα Origen uses this concept to argue that the prophets were not deceived by daemonic illusions, but really saw divine realities. It also serves the apologetic purpose of emphasizing the prophets' intellectual capabilities. Their minds are so turned towards God that they see, hear, taste, and touch divine truth. Only those with such sharpened intellectual powers are able to know God, while the Greeks who are concerned with the oracles and idol-worship have become blinded in the eye of the soul.

Origen argues that the mark of the true prophet is thus an increase in rationality. Concerning the Hebrew prophets, he says, "Because of the touch, so to speak, of what is called the Holy Spirit upon their soul they possessed clear mental vision" (*Cels.* 7.4). He asserts, against the prophetic ecstasy experienced by the Pythian oracle, that inspiration, instead of removing the mind of the prophet, actually augments it. He says,

> The person inspired by the divine spirit ought to have derived from it far more benefit than anyone who may be instructed by the oracles. ... And for that reason he ought to possess the clearest vision at the very time when the deity is in communion with him.[56]

The true prophet can thus be identified by his wisdom, spiritual insight, and heightened rationality.

---

[56]*Cels.* 7.3. Völker argues that Origen was a proponent of ecstasy, and that for Origen, ecstatic union made absolute knowledge of God possible on earth. However, Völker dismisses this passage from the *Against Celsus* as untrustworthy because of the apologetic context, and likewise discards passages from *On First Principles* on the grounds of Rufinus' translation. Crouzel has shown that Völker is mistaken on this issue. Völker, *Vollkommenheitsideal*, pp. 138-141; Crouzel, *La "connaissance mystique,"* pp. 202-208.

This is what Origen means by saying that the prophets had received divine inspiration. In reality, says Origen, they had, by a rigorous life of virtue, and a persistent turning away from the flesh and raising of their eyes to God, received a share in divinity. What Chadwick usually translated as "inspired," or "divinely inspired" Origen uses in a somewhat stronger sense. The prophets participated in, and received a share of, divinity. Moses was not a γόης, but μετέχων θειοτέρου πνεύματος (*Cels.* 3.5). The prophets possessed τὸ θεῖον (*Cels.* 4.34), and τῆς θείας κατακωχῆς (*Cels.* 7.7), and were φίλοι θεοῦ (*Cels.* 4.3), and δεκτικοὶ τοῦ θείου πνεύματος (*Cels.* 4.7). They could not possibly be deceived by the daemons, because in the power of their virtuous lives, and the participation in divinity, they were well above the circles of daemonic influence. Indeed, people with that sort of spiritual power are able to cast out daemons.

Origen is thus just as aware as Celsus of the ambiguities of inspiration, and the danger involved in prophecy. Like Celsus, he believes that those who are inordinately concerned with the things of this world easily become entrapped by the hostile daemonic world which surrounds and infiltrates all of human life. The question of prophetic experience is thus a crucial one: were the prophets daemonic or divine? In response to Celsus' attack on the Christian reliance upon prophecy, Origen is concerned, then, not to simply re-assert the argument of fulfillment of prophecy, but to defend the nature of the prophets' experience. To Celsus' charges of daemon-involvement and delusion by phantasms, Origen responds that the Old Testament prophets were in fact well on their way in the ascent of the soul to God, and well beyond the restraining influence of the daemons. The marks of the success of their ascent were their virtue, which surpassed that of all their contemporaries, and their rationality, which lifted up their minds to God and enabled them to see with a 'divine sense.' Like Celsus, Origen is concerned with the sources of spiritual power, and means of spiritual combat, and he shares Celsus' concern for freedom from the spiritual forces which ensnare the soul. For Origen, the divine power of the Christian message, imparted to divine men by a divine spirit, provides the means for the ascent of the soul.

CONCLUSION

A debate has been underway for over half a century concerning the nature of Origen's thought. The question which has occupied Origen scholars is whether Origen should be considered a rationalist or a mystic in his approach to the knowledge of God. On the one hand, Eugene de Faye's treatment presented Origen as a philosopher, little influenced by distinctively Christian or biblical themes, who produced a speculative system.[57] On the other hand, Walther Völker created somewhat of a sensation when he argued that Origen was a mystic of the first order, who believed in irrational ecstasies and the possibility of absolute knowledge of God in this life by means of complete union with divinity.[58]

Each of these viewpoints has had its champions. Hal Koch has taken the side of de Faye, and extended de Faye's work in his own. For Koch, Origen, while not a cold rationalist, is a systematician who sees God and the Logos primarily as educators. Koch says that Völker's concept of Origen as a mystic is simply wrong, and that one must choose between the mystical and rationalist characterizations of Origen.[59] On the other hand, Henri Crouzel has questioned the intellectual picture of de Faye and Koch, and while noting the intellectual and speculative concerns of Origen, argues that Origen's motivation is in fact spiritual and mystical. Crouzel says,

> Une grande erudition, sacrée et profane, peut aider à voir la volonté de la Parole de Dieu, mais le but est d'entrer dans la pensée divine et de l'incorporer à tout son être. Le côté intellectuel est secondaire et subordonné.[60]

---

[57]De Faye, *Origène*, cited by Völker, *Vollkommenheitsideal*, p. 13.

[58]Völker, *Vollkommenheitsideal*.

[59]Koch, *Pronoia und Paideusis*, p. 342.

[60]Crouzel, *La "connaissance mystique,"* p. 532. Most recently, Joseph W. Trigg has mediated somewhat between these two positions. Trigg sees Origen as a "charismatic intellectual," who is oriented towards the church and has a

Crouzel, however, although he takes sides in this debate, notes the artificiality of these distinctions. He says, "Cette opposition si tranchée est artificelle. . . . Le mélange de spéculation et de mystique fait-il vraiment problème?"[61] The difficulties raised by such an opposition indicate that categories and concerns are being introduced which are not intrinsic to the thought of Origen or antiquity. From our examination of the debate between Celsus and Origen it is clear that the issues of mysticism or intellectualism do not occupy them; what is central to the debate is the question of spiritual power and freedom. The apologetic context is thus very enlightening; the *Against Celsus* focuses on the concerns central to both pagan and Christian, and the debate over prophecy is one of the most important of these concerns. This conflict addresses a pressing spiritual issue of its world: which side has the spiritual effectiveness sufficient to break the encompassing power of the daemons and to make available the knowledge of God?

---

charismatic understanding of church ministry and exegesis, but who sees the ultimate charism as knowledge and a heightening of the intellect. Joseph W. Trigg, "The Charismatic Intellectual: Origen's Understanding of Religious Leadership," *Church History* 50 (1981):5-19.

[61]Crouzel, La *"connaissance mystique,"* p. 532.

Chapter 6

Conclusion

> We have here concluded in eight books
> everything which we thought fit to say in
> reply to Celsus' book. . . . It is for the reader
> of his treatise, and of our reply against him,
> to judge which of the two breathes more of
> the spirit of the true God and of the temper of
> devotion towards Him and of the truth
> attainable by men, that is, of sound doctrines
> which lead men to live the best life. *Origen
> Cels. 8.76.*

Christians were known in the ancient world for their reliance on
prophecy and inspiration. Celsus said they took the prophecies of the
Jews, and could even be called "Sibyllists" because of their pilfering of
Greek prophecy (*Cels.* 5.62). This reliance depended on the antiquity of
the prophecies and their fulfillment in the present. However, our
examination of the polemic of Celsus and Origen has indicated a deeper
stream of discussion, which tapped into powerful themes of late antique
thought. The debate over prophecy was the debate over the sources of
inspiration, and ultimately, over the source of the spiritual power
necessary to evade the restraining forces of human life, and to succeed in
coming to the knowledge of divine truth. The late antique world was
one whose citizens were aware of the spiritual power of both the
heavenly and the more ambiguous earthly regions. According to Peter
Brown, "The 'earthly' region, therefore, was never neutral. Men had to
make up their minds about bearers of 'heavenly' power in an

environment heavy with alternative, if invisible, 'earthly' sources of power."[1]

This study of the role of prophecy in the polemic of the ancient world has shown that it is these types of issues which are at work in the struggles between pagan and Christian. Pagan understandings of prophecy, inspiration and revelation provided the theory and language for the discussion of the experience of prophecy, visions, dreams, and the knowledge of God. The background of second-century Christian apologetic indicates how Christian understandings of the daemonic world, prophecy, and the character of the prophet were used in the Christian announcement of the freedom to be found in the Logos.

Celsus stands as an heir of both these traditions; as a Platonist he is familiar with current philosophical treatment of the issue, and as an informed polemicist, he replies to contemporary Christian arguments. Origen's response provides an illuminating example of the importance of this issue in the late antique world, for as a philosopher, Christian, and mystic, he displays a practical concern for the issues of spiritual freedom and power.

The hellenistic context demonstrates a wide-ranging discussion of prophecy which provides the foundation for the apologetic context in both paganism and Christianity. In general, prophecy is the source of much debate, but is considered to be a power of the soul, actuated by the movements of various forces. For most thinkers, the soul possesses a kinship with the divine which calls it upward, and makes possible a measure of divine knowledge. For Plato, *eros* is the most potent inspiration, and Platonists after him, such as Philo, speak of the heavenward yearning of the soul. Prophecy itself is considered to be a faculty of the soul, which, like memory, is able to provide the soul with knowledge of non-present reality. The prophetic faculty is seen as a blank slate or mirror, waiting to reflect the images produced in it, and prophecy is held to consist of images and representations impressed on the prophetic faculty by the inspiring force. This force can be the movement of the inquiring soul itself, inspiration by the divine, or the impressions on the soul caused by daemons. These daemons, entrusted with the providential care of the earth, are, for the most part, viewed in

---

[1] Brown, *The Making of Late Antiquity,* p. 18.

a positive light. The primary factor hindering prophecy is the body, which holds the soul down with its earthly needs and desires. The needs of the body confuse and darken the inspiration received from gods or daemons.

This view of prophecy is applied in the polemic surrounding the claims of extraordinary figures such as Apollonius of Tyana. The major concern of such apologetic is to demonstrate that the prophet has successfully escaped the downward strain of the body and lower influences, and achieved his foreknowledge by the communion of his soul with the divine. The charges against such figures attempt to show that they have not succeeded in rising above the hindering influences. Their oracles are accused of ambiguity and obscurity, they are charged with sorcery, and with involvement with lower spirits and the accompanying deception of their visions and apparitions. In response to such charges, the ascetic discipline and purity of soul of the prophet are displayed, and a figure such as Apollonius protests that he is a σόφος, not a μάντις. The ethical concern thus predominates, since knowledge of God is achieved by the successful withdrawal of the soul from the body and the lifting of the eye of the soul. The chief obstacle to true prophecy lies in the soul itself and its connection with the body. Daemons are viewed as intermediate agents of providence, and as such, are sources of inspiration. While they are less than divine, they are not predominantly evil, and are not generally a threat to prophetic knowledge, at least not to those whose souls are properly prepared.

While this understanding of prophecy was common to hellenistic thinking, the Christians introduced a new feature into the discussion of prophecy. Drawing upon Jewish demonology and apologetic, the Christian apologists asserted that behind the apparent accomplishments of Greek literature and culture lay not divine inspiration, but the activity of lower spiritual beings who were hostile to humanity. The earthly daemons had waged a campaign of deceptive inspiration to prevent the human race from rising above their influence, and had kept it bound to earth. This argument, in the apologetic context, amounted to a redefinition of human society; nearly all that had gone before was an enslaving tactic of daemons, and truth and freedom were to be found only among those who had been enlightened to daemonic influence, that is, the Christians.

For Justin and the other apologists, the manifestations of this enslavement were to be found in the errors of the philosophers, the licentiousness of the poets, and the impiety of idolatry. However, this enslavement had a more personal character as well. All of those who participated in daemonic culture acquired an evil daemon of their own, a daemonic familiar, and much of the evil of human nature was due to the impulses of one's attending daemon. The daemons took an active hand in inspiration, moving human beings to wickedness, and providing apparitions and phantasms to delude them.

The polemic which surrounds the extraordinary figures of the Christians, however, is similar to that of the pagan world. For both groups, the prophet must be one who ascended beyond the enslaving influences of the lower world, and many of the charges which are leveled at Apollonius of Tyana are directed at Simon Magus and Marcus in the Christian camp. Sorcery provides the main grounds of accusation; the false prophet achieves his foreknowledge by his magical skill, rather than by receiving it from the Holy Spirit. Involvement with lower spirits is an equally potent charge; the false prophet has a familiar daemon, or calls upon spirits to send him dreams. Dependence upon visions, phantasms, and apparitions is also a sign of daemonic influence. The true prophet is filled with the Holy Spirit, and receives knowledge, not visions or apparitions.

The issue here, as with the pagans, is freedom from lower, earthly influences. The true prophet is a sage, or one who has knowledge of God because of the successful ascent of his soul from the earthly realm to the heavenly. In much the same way as Apollonius, the Peter of the Clementine literature protests that foreknowledge does not come intermittently in trances or dreams, but lies within the soul of the wise man. The predominant spiritual concerns evident in the issue of prophecy are freedom from the enslaving forces of the lower spiritual powers, and finding knowledge untainted by their influences.

Celsus, often touted as a rationalist, criticizes Christianity in such a way as to make clear that he sees the issue in these terms. Unlike many of the earlier pagan discussions of prophecy, Celsus takes up the Christian attack on hellenistic culture with an equal concern for the misleading influence of the daemons. He argues, however, that it is the Christians, rather than the Greeks, who have been deceived. Celsus shares the common philosophical view of the daemons as intermediaries between mortal and divine, and of their role as overseers of the world. However, he agrees with the Christians that the daemons of the earthly sphere, entrenched as they are in lower, earthly concerns, entangle those who consort with them in the material world, frustrating the soul's efforts to rise to God. This, he says, is what has happened to the Christians. Their prophets, as well as Christ their founder, were unsuccessful in rising above the lower daemonic influence, they were thus entrapped by earthly daemons, and remained ignorant of divine truth. The fleshly character of Christian doctrine and the daemonic involvement of such Christian groups as the Ophites are evidence of this entrapment. Celsus uses the kind of polemic we have seen to demonstrate his point concerning the daemonic involvement of the Christian prophets: Moses and Jesus were sorcerers, rather than sages, and the prophecy of the Old Testament, as well as contemporary Christian prophecy, is ambiguous and confused. A sure sign of Christian failure to penetrate the daemonic veil is their reliance upon apparitions and visions; the Gnostics court phantasms, and the miracles and post-resurrection appearances of Jesus were simply apparitions.

Although the concern for freedom from daemonic forces and spiritual power is found in various forms in second- century thought, Celsus, the well-informed critic of the Christians, seems to have been influenced by his Christian opponents in this respect. Unlike many of his predecessors, Celsus agrees that the daemonic realm can be a source of confusion and deception for the soul. Aware of the attacks of Christian apologetic upon Greek culture, Celsus replies in kind. He accepts the premise that inspiration is a dangerous thing, often manipulated by the daemons, but argues that it is the Christians, not the Greeks, who have suffered from this manipulation. The issue between them is not the task of the soul seeking God, or the dangers confronting it, but that of which group has succeeded in overcoming these dangers.

Origen places this issue even more squarely in the context of spiritual conflict. His understanding of inspiration and prophecy is tied closely to his view of the ascent of the soul, and thus is near the center of his thought. For Origen, the unaided soul is unable to attain knowledge of God, and inspiration and divine grace are needed. The human soul, however, is open to daemonic as well as divine influences, and daemons are able to exert wicked force on the imagination and the ruling power of the mind. The free will makes the choice between the influences of the divine and daemonic, and human history is the story of the persuasive efforts of the Logos and the perverting efforts of the daemons. God has been in a process of educating human souls, and the daemons have been attempting to keep them bound in the material realm.

For Origen, virtue is the means of victory in this spiritual combat. Inspiration, divine grace, and knowledge of God are given according to merit, to those who have rejected the material impulses of the daemons and have lifted the eye of the soul to God. The reward of the progress in virtue is divine illumination, or an increase and enlightenment of the intellectual powers of the soul. Like Philo, Origen portrays the wise man as possessing all the Stoic virtues, but unlike Philo, he rejects ecstasy as the spiritual summit, and argues that the mind, rather than being taken out of itself, is elevated and illuminated.

This, for Origen, is the experience of the prophets. Against Celsus' charges of daemonic involvement and prophetic deception, Origen asserts that the prophets stand at the pinnacle of spiritual progress, and see divine truth clearly and brilliantly. They have so participated in divinity as to possess 'divine senses,' and rather than being deceived by daemonic phantasms, have actually perceived divine truth. Origen agrees that false prophets are deceived by the daemons, but asserts that the founders of Christianity have attained the victory in this spiritual warfare, and, as divine and inspired men, received and proclaimed the true knowledge of God.

This study has surveyed the polemic surrounding the issue of prophecy between Greek and Christian. In doing so, it has noted the significant terms of the conflict, and the exchange of charges such as sorcery, ambiguity, obscurity, φάσμα and φαντασία. It has noted as well the places of Celsus and Origen in their respective traditions on this subject. More importantly, however, two features of antique thought have been demonstrated. First, it is evident that prophecy is central to the debate between pagan and Christian. Scholars in the past have well noted the Christian arguments from the fulfillment of prophecy and the antiquity of the Old Testament prophets, but there has been little attention paid to the issue of inspiration and the experience of the prophets themselves. This study, however, has shown that it can no longer be said, as Gustave Bardy said of Origen, that there was no interest in the psychology of the prophet. The issue of true and false prophecy was at the center of the clash of two ways of viewing the world and society, with each side claiming that the highest values of the other were in reality the product of daemonic inspiration. The question of the locus of divine truth often became that of where were people with souls divine enough to acquire and guarantee truth. Thus the souls of the prophets were the subject of intense scrutiny and polemic. Beyond the clash of cultures, the concern for personal spiritual warfare focused on this issue as well. The problem of ambiguous and malevolent inspiration was of great significance to a culture in which one of the largest personal concerns was how to deal with those forces which affect human life. The question of spiritual power and freedom, as many have recently pointed out, was one which occupied pagan and Christian alike. The apologetic debate over prophecy was often conducted in these terms; the question was that of which side possessed the spiritual power and knowledge to overcome those forces limiting human life.

Second, this study has indicated the place of Celsus and Origen in this culture. Most modern treatments of both Celsus and Origen have attempted to deal with them in terms of modern questions: those of rationalism vs. fideism, philosophy vs. superstition, intellectualism vs. mysticism. The limits of this approach have been demonstrated in the examination of the issue of prophecy. Both Origen and Celsus are philosophers, yet they do not share the modern distinctions between intellectualism and mysticism or religious practice. Rather, they are motivated by the issue of their age, the soul's ascent to God, and how to deal with the obstacles to that ascent. In treating this issue, they bring to bear a consistent view of the cosmos and humanity's place within it. Both saw the cosmos in terms of the human soul's struggle to defeat the forces restraining it, and each had a set of similar, but not coextensive, criteria for judging various attempts in this struggle. These criteria did not include those of rationalism and mysticism, but rather the values common to their age, those of the soul and the heavenly realm. They were both citizens as well as shapers of their age, and both were concerned with the soul, its spiritual enemies, and its ultimate freedom and enlightenment.

Bibliography

PRIMARY SOURCES

Editions

Clement of Alexandria. *Le Pédagogue.* Edited by Henri-Irenée Marrou. 3 vols. Sources Chrétiennes no. 70, 108, 158. Paris: Editions du Cerf, 1960-1970.

Clementine Homilies and Recognitions. Patrologiae cursus completus. Series Graecae. Edited by J. P. Migne. *Homilies*, vol. 2, col. 57-468. *Recognitions*, vol. 2, col. 1171-1454.

Corpus apologetarum Christianorum saeculi secundi. Edited by Ioann. Carol. Theod. Otto. Iena: Frider. Mauke, 1847-1861. Vol. 1, *Iustini opera (1 and 2 Apology, Dialogue with Trypho).* Vol. 2, *Opera Iustini addubitata (Exhortation to the Greeks).* Vol. 6, *Tatiani opera (Address to the Greeks).* Vol. 7, *Athenagorae opera (Plea for the Christians).* Vol. 8, *Theophili Ad Autolycum.*

Epiphanius. Pierre de Labriolle, *Les sources de l'histoire du montanisme; textes Grecs, Latins, Syriaques.* Fribourg: Librairie de l'universite, 1913.

Hermas. *Le Pasteur.* Edited by Robert Joly. Sources Chrétiennes no. 53. Paris: Editions du Cerf, 1958.

Irenaeus. *Sancti Irenaeus libros quinque adversus haereses.* Edited by W. Wigan Harvey. 2 vols. Cambridge: Cambridge University Press, 1857.

Lucian of Samosata. *Lucian in Eight Volumes.* Translated by A. M. Harmon. Vol. 6, *Alexander the False Prophet.* Loeb Classical Library. Cambridge: Harvard University Press, 1953.

Origen. *Origenes Werke.* Edited by Paul Koetschau. Leipzig: J. C. Hinrichs, 1899-1919. Vols. 1 and 2, *Contra Celsum*; vol. 5, *De principiis.*

145

Philo. *Philo in Ten Volumes.* Translated by F. H. Colson and G. H. Whitaker. Cambridge: Harvard University Press, 1958. Loeb Classical Library. Vol. 4, *On the Migration of Abraham, Who is the Heir of Divine Things.* Vol. 5, *On Dreams, That They are God-Sent.* Vol. 6, *The Life of Moses.*

Philostratus. *Life of Apollonius of Tyana.* Translated by F. C. Conybeare. Loeb Classical Library. Cambridge: Harvard University Press, 1948.

Plato. *Plato in Twelve Volumes.* Cambridge: Harvard University Press, 1977, first printed, 1914. Loeb Classical Library. Vol. 1, *Euthyphro, Apology, Crito, Phaedo, Phaedrus.* Edited by Harold North Fowler. Vol. 9, *Timaeus, Critias, Cleitophon, Menexenus, Epistles.* Translated by R. G. Bury.

Plutarch. *Plutarch's Moralia.* Loeb Classical Library. Cambridge: Harvard University Press, 1960. Vol. 5, *Isis and Osiris, The E at Delphi, Oracles at Delphi No Longer Given in Verse, The Obsolescence of Oracles.* Translated by Frank Cole Babbitt. Vol. 7, *The Genius of Socrates.* Translated by Phillip H. De Lacy and Benedict Einarson.

Tertullian. *Apology, De spectaculis.* Translated by T. R. Glover. Loeb Classical Library. Cambridge: Harvard University Press, 1960.

_____. *Tertulliani de anima.* Edited by J. H. Waszink. Amsterdam: J. M. Meulenhoff, 1947.

Translations

The Ante-Nicene Fathers. Edited by Alexander Roberts and James Donaldson. Revised by A. Cleveland Coxe. American reprint of the Edinburgh Edition. Grand Rapids: William B. Eerdmans, 1977. Vol. 1, *The Apostolic Fathers with Justin Martyr and Irenaeus.* Vol. 2, *Fathers of the Second Century: Hermas, Tatian, Athenagoras, Theophilus, and Clement of Alexandria.* Vol. 3, *Latin Christianity: Its Founder, Tertullian.* Vol. 8, *Twelve Patriarchs, Excerpts and Epistles, The Clementina, Apocrypha, Decretals, Memories of Edessa and Syriac Documents, Remains of the First Ages.*

Lucian of Samosata. *Lucian in Eight Volumes.* Translated by A. M. Harmon. Vol. 6, *Alexander the False Prophet.* Loeb Classical Library. Cambridge: Harvard University Press, 1953.

Origen. *Origen on First Principles*. Translated by G. W. Butterworth. London: Society for Promoting Christian Knowledge, 1936. Reprint edition, Gloucester, Mass.: Peter Smith, 1973.

_____. *Contra Celsum*. Translated by Henry Chadwick. Cambridge: Cambridge University Press, 1953. Reprint edition, 1980.

Philo. *Philo in Ten Volumes*. Translated by F. H. Colson and G. H. Whitaker. Cambridge: Harvard University Press, 1958. Loeb Classical Library. Vol. 4, *On the Migration of Abraham, Who is the Heir of Divine Things*. Vol. 5, *On Dreams, That They are God-Sent*. Vol. 6, *The Life of Moses*.

Philostratus. *Life of Apollonius of Tyana*. Translated by F. C. Conybeare. Loeb Classical Library. Cambridge: Harvard University Press, 1948.

Plato. *Plato in Twelve Volumes*. Cambridge: Harvard University Press, 1977, first printed, 1914. Loeb Classical Library. Vol. 1, *Euthyphro, Apology, Crito, Phaedo, Phaedrus*. Edited by Harold North Fowler. Vol. 9, *Timaeus, Critias, Cleitophon, Menexenus, Epistles*. Translated by R. G. Bury.

Plutarch. *Plutarch's Moralia*. Loeb Classical Library. Cambridge: Harvard University Press, 1960. Vol. 5, *Isis and Osiris, The E at Delphi, Oracles at Delphi No Longer Given in Verse, The Obsolescence of Oracles*. Translated by Frank Cole Babbitt. Vol. 7, *The Genius of Socrates*. Translated by Phillip H. De Lacy and Benedict Einarson.

Tertullian. *Apology, De Spectaculis*. Translated by T. R. Glover. Loeb Classical Library. Cambridge: Harvard University Press, 1960.

SECONDARY LITERATURE

Andresen, Carl. *Logos und Nomos: Die Polemik des Kelsos wider das Christentum*. Arbeiten zur Kirkengeschichte, 30. Berlin: De Gruyter, 1955.

Arbesmann, Rudolf. "Fasting and Prophecy in Pagan and Christian Antiquity." *Traditio* 7 (1949-1951):1-71.

Armstrong, A. Hilary. "Pagan and Christian Traditionalism in the First Three Centuries A.D." *Studia Patristica* 15 (1984):414-431.

_____. "The Self-Definition of Christianity in Relation to Later Platonism." In *Jewish and Christian Self-Definition*. 3 vols. Philadelphia: Fortress Press, 1982. Vol. 1, *The Shaping of Christianity in the Second and Third Centuries*. Edited by E. P. Sanders.

Aune, David. "Herm. Man. 11.2: Christian False Prophets Who Say What People Wish to Hear." *Journal of Biblical Literature* 97 (1978):103-104.

_____. "The Odes of Solomon and Early Christian Prophecy." *New Testament Studies* 28 (1982):435-460.

_____. *Prophecy in Early Christianity and the Ancient Mediterranean World*. Grand Rapids: William B. Eerdmans, 1983.

Bader, Robert. *Der Ἀληθης Λόγος des Kelsos*. Tübinger Beiträge zur Altertumswissenschaft, H. 33. Stuttgart: W. Kohlhammer, 1940.

Bardy, Gustave. "La spiritualite d'Origène." *Supplement à La vie spirituelle* 31 (1932):80-106.

_____. "Origène et le magie." *Recherches de science religieuse* 18 (1928):126-142.

Barnes, Timothy. *Tertullian: A Historical and Literary Study*. Oxford: Clarendon Press, 1971.

Behr, C. A. *Aelius Aristides and the Sacred Tales*. Amsterdam: Hakkert, 1968.

Bevan, Edwyn. *Sibyls and Seers*. London: Allen and Unwin, 1928.

Bieler, Ludwig. *ΘΕΙΟΣ ΑΝΗΡ: Das Bild des göttlichen Menschen in Spätantike und Frühchristentum*. Darmstadt: Wissenschaftliche Buchgesellschaft, 1967. First published 1935-36.

Bigg, Charles. *The Christian Platonists of Alexandria*. Oxford: Clarendon Press, 1913.

Bjorck, G. "Onar Idein: De la perception de la rêve chez les anciens." *Eranos* 44 (1946):306-314.

Blanc, Cécile. "L'angélogie d'Origène." *Studia Patristica* 14 (1975/76):243-256.

Boer, W. den. "La polémique anti-chrétienne du IIe siècle: 'La doctrine de vérité' de Celse." *Athenaeum* n.s. 54 (1976):300-318.

Bonner, Campbell. "Some Phases of Religious Feeling in Later Paganism." *Harvard Theological Review* 30 (1937):119-140.

Borret, Marcel, ed. *Origène: Contre Celse*. Tome 5, Introduction generale, tables et index. Sources Chrétiennes, no. 227. Paris: Editions du Cerf, 1976.

Boyancé, Pierre. "Les deux démons personnels dans l'antiquité Grecque et Latin." *Revue de philologie* 3rd series 9 (1935):189-202.

Brenk, F. E. *In Mists Apparelled: Religious Themes in Plutarch's Moralia and Lives*. Mnemosyne, supplement no. 48. Leiden: Brill, 1977.

Brown, Peter. *The Making of Late Antiquity*. Cambridge: Harvard University Press, 1978.

_____. "Sorcery, Demons, and the Rise of Christianity from Late Antiquity into the Middle Ages." In *Witchcraft Confessions and Accusations*, p. 17-45. Edited by Mary Douglas. A.S.A. Monographs no. 9. London: Tavistock, 1970.

Burke, Gary T. "Celsus and the Old Testament." *Vetus Testamentum* 36 (1986):241-245.

_____. "Walter Bauer and Celsus: The Shape of Late Second-Century Christianity." *The Second Century* 4 (1984):1-7.

Cadiou, René. "Origène et les 'reconnaissances clémentines'." *Recherches de science religieuse* 20 (1930):506-528.

Chadwick, Henry. "The Evidences of Christianity in the Apologetic of Origen." *Studia Patristica* 2 (1951):331-339.

_____. "Justin Martyr's Defence of Christianity." *Bulletin of the John Rylands Library* 47 (1964):275-297.

_____. "Origen, Celsus, and the Stoa." *Journal of Theological Studies* 48 (1947):34-49.

Cornford, Francis M. *Plato's Cosmology: The Timaeus of Plato*. Indianapolis: Bobbs-Merrill, reprint.

Cox, Patricia. "Origen and the Witch of Endor: Toward an Iconoclastic Typology." *Anglican Theological Review* 66 (1984):137-147.

Crouzel, Henri. "L'anthropologie d'Origène dans la perspective du combat spirituel." *Revue d'ascetique et de mystique* 31 (1955):364-385.

_____. "Conviction intérieure et aspects extérieurs de la religion chez Celse et Origène." *Bulletin de littérature ecclesiastique* 77 (1976):81-98.

_____. *Origène et la "connaissance mystique"*. Paris: De Brouwer, 1961.

_____. "Les prophéties de la résurrection selon Origène." In *Forma Futuri: Studi in onore del Cardinale Michele Pellegrino*, pp. 980-992. Torino: Bottega d'Erasmo, 1975.

_____. "Le thème platonicien du 'vehicle de l'âme' chez Origène." *Didaskalia* 7 (1977):225-238.

_____. *Théologie de l'image de Dieu chez Origène*. Aubier: Editions Montaigne, 1956.

Culianu, Joan P. "Le vol magique dans l'antiquitie tardive." *Revue de l'histoire des religions* 198 (1981):57-66.

Cumont, Franz. *Astrology and Religion Among the Greeks and Romans*. First published, 1912; reprint ed., New York: Dove, 1960.

Daniélou, Jean. *The Development of Christian Doctrine before the Council of Nicea*. Vol. 1: *The Theology of Jewish Christianity*. Translated by John A. Baker. London: Dartman, Longman, & Todd, 1964.

_____. *Origen*. New York: Sheed & Ward, 1955.

_____. *Philon d'Alexandrie*. Paris: Librairie Artheme Fayard, 1958.

Davies, W.D. *Paul and Rabbinic Judaism: Some Rabbinic Elements in Pauline Theology*. Revised edition. New York: Harper, 1953.

Dillon, John. *The Middle Platonists, 80 B.C. to A.D. 220*. Ithaca, NY: Cornell University Press, 1977.

Dodds, E. R. *The Greeks and the Irrational*. Berkeley: University of California Press, 1951.

_____. *Pagan and Christian in an Age of Anxiety*. New York: W. W. Norton, 1965.

Dölger, Franz Joseph. "Teufels Großmutter: *Magna Mater Deum* und *Magna Mater Daemonum*." *Antike und Christentum* 3 (1932):153-176.

_____. "ΘΕΟΥ ΦΩΝΗ: Die 'Gottes-Stimme' bei Ignatius von Antiochien, Kelsos und Origenes." *Antike und Christentum* 5 (1936):218-223.

Dörrie, Heinrich. "Die platonische Theologie des Kelsos in ihrer Auseinandersetzung mit der christlichen Theologie, auf Grund von Origenes c. Celsum 7.42 ff." *Nachrichten der Akademie der Wissenschaften in Göttingen*. I. Philologische-historische Klasse, 1967, pp. 23-55.

Dulaey, Martine. *Le rêve dans la vie et la pensée de Saint Augustin*. Paris: Etudes Augustiniennes, 1973.

Fascher, Eric. *PROPHETES: Eine sprach- und religionsgeschichtliche Untersuchung*. Gießen: A. Töpelmann, 1927.

Faye, Eugene de. *Origen and His Work*. Translated by Fred Rothwell. New York: Columbia University Press, 1929.

_____. *Origène, sa vie, son oeuvre, sa pensée*. Paris: Editions E. Leroux, 1923-28.

Feldman, Louis H. "Josephus as an Apologist to the Greco-Roman World: His Portrait of Solomon." In *Aspects of Religious Propaganda in Judaism and Early Christianity*, pp. 69-98. Edited by Elisabeth Schüssler Fiorenza. Notre Dame: University of Notre Dame Press, 1976.

Festugière, André Jean. *La révélation d'Hermes Trismégiste*. 4 vols. Paris: Librairie Lecoffre, 1954.

Fiorenza, Elisabeth Schüssler. "Miracles, Mission and Apologetic: An Introduction." In *Aspects of Religious Propaganda in Judaism and Early Christianity*, pp. 1-25. Edited by Elisabeth Schüssler Fiorenza. Notre Dame: University of Notre Dame Press, 1976.

Flacelière, Robert. *Greek Oracles*. Translated by Douglas Garman. New York: W.W. Norton, 1965.

_____. "La delire de la Pythie: est-il un liquide?" *Revue des etudes Augustiniennes* 52 (1950):315-324.

Gager, John G. *Moses in Greco-Roman Paganism*. Nashville: Abingdon Press, 1972.

Gallagher, Eugene V. *Divine Man or Magician?: Celsus and Origen on Jesus*. Society of Biblical Literature Dissertation Series no. 64. Chico, Ca.: Scholars Press, 1982.

Geffcken, Johannes. *Zwei griechische Apologeten*. Leipzig, 1907; reprint ed., Hildesheim: Georg Olms, 1970.

Glöckner, Otto. *Celsi ΑΛΗΘΗΣ ΛΟΓΟΣ*. Kleine Texte für Vorlesungen und Übungen. Bonn: Marcus und E. Webers Verlag, 1924.

_____. "Die Gottes- und Weltanschauung des Celsus." *Philologus* 82, neue Folge 36 (1927):329-352.

Goldin, Judah. "The Magic of Magic and Superstition." In *Aspects of Religious Propaganda in Judaism and Early Christianity*, pp. 115-147. Edited by Elisabeth Schüssler Fiorenza. Notre Dame: University of Notre Dame Press, 1976.

Grant, Robert M. *Greek Apologists of the Second Century*. Philadelphia: Westminster, 1988.

_____. *The Letter and the Spirit*. London: SPCK, 1957.

_____. *Miracle and Natural Law in Greco-Roman and Early Christian Thought*. Amsterdam: North Holland, 1952.

Guillaumont, François. *Philosophe et augure. Recherches sur la théorie Cicéronienne de la divination*. Bruxelles: Latomus, 1984.

Harl, Marguerite. "La 'bouche' et le 'coeur' de l'apotre. Deux images biblique du 'sens divin' de l'homme (Proverbes 2,5) chez Origène." In *Forma Futuri: Studi in onore del Cardinal Michele Pelligrino*, pp. 17-42. Torino: Bottega d'Erasmo, 1975.

_____. "La langage de l'experience religieuse chez les pères Grecs." *Revista di storia et litteratura religiosa* 13 (1977):5-34.

_____. *Origène et la fonction révélatrice du Verbe incarné*. Paris: Editions du Seuil, 1958.

Harnack, Adolf. *The Mission and Expansion of Christianity in the First Three Centuries*. Translated by James Moffat. 2nd. ed. Theological Translation Library, vol. 19 and 20. London: Williams & Norgate, 1908.

Hauck, Robert J. "*Omnes contra Celsum*." *The Second Century* 5 (1985/86):211-225.

_____. "'They Saw What They Said They Said They Saw': Sense Knowledge in Early Christian Polemic." *Harvard Theological Review* 81 (1988):239-249.

Headlam, A. C. "The Clementine Literature." *Journal of Theological Studies* 3 (1901-2):41-58.

Henry, P. "Plutarch and Origen on Theology and Language." *Studia Patristica* 15 (1984):453-457.

Hoffmann, R. Joseph. *Celsus: On the True Doctrine*. New York: Oxford University Press, 1987.

Holladay, Carl H. *Theios Aner in Hellenistic Judaism: A Critique of the Use of This Category in New Testament Christology*. Society of Biblical Literature Dissertation Series no. 40. Missoula, Montana: Scholars Press, 1977.

Holmes, Michael "Origen and the Inerrancy of Scripture." *Journal of the Evangelical Theological Society* 24 (1981):221-231.

Irmscher, J. "The Pseudo-Clementines." In *New Testament Apocrypha*, vol. 2, pp. 532-535. Edited by Edgar Hennecke, Wilhelm Schneelmelcher, R. McL. Wilson. Philadelphia: Westminster Press, 1965.

Joly, Robert. "Hermas et le Pasteur." *Vigiliae Christianae* 21 (1967):201-208.

Jones, F. Stanley. "The Pseudo-Clementines: A History of Research." *The Second Century* 2 (1982):1-33, 63-96.

Kee, Howard Clark. *Medicine, Miracle and Magic in New Testament Times.* Cambridge: Cambridge University Press, 1986.

_____. *Miracle in the Early Christian World: A Study in Sociohistorical Model.* New Haven: Yale University Press, 1983.

Keim, Theodor. *Kelsos/Celsus. Wahres Wort. Älteste Streitschrift antiker Weltanschauung gegen das Christentum.* Darmstadt: Aalen, 1969. First published 1873.

Koch, Hal. *Pronoia und Paideusis: Studien über Origenes und sein Verhaltnis zum Platonismus.* Arbeiten zur Kirchengeschichte 22. New York: Garland, 1979. First published Berlin: De Gruyter & Co., 1932.

Kolenkow, A. B. "A Problem of Power: How Miracle-Doers Counter Charges of Magic in the Hellenistic World." *Society of Biblical Literature 1976 Seminar Papers: One Hundred Twelfth Annual Meeting,* pp. 105-111. Missoula, Montana: Scholars Press.

Kydd, Ronald. "Origen and the Gifts of the Spirit." *Eglise et théologie* 13 (1982):111-116.

Labriolle, Pierre de. *La réaction païenne: Etude sur la polémique antichrétienne du Ier au VIe siècle.* 8th ed. Paris: L'artisan du livre, 1934.

Lane Fox, Robin. *Pagans and Christians.* New York: Alfred A. Knopf, 1987.

Latourelle, René. "L'idée de révélation chez les pères de l'Eglise." *Sciences ecclesiastique* 11 (1959):297-344.

Lebreton, Jules. "Les degrees de la connaissance religieuse d'après Origène." *Recherches de science religieuse* 12 (1922):265-296.

Lejay, Paul. "La plectre, la langue, et l'Esprit." *Bulletin d'ancienne littérature et d'archeologie chrétienne* 2 (1912):43-45.

Lewis, I.M. *Ecstatic Religion: An Anthropological Study of Spirit Possession and Shamanism.* New York: Penguin, 1971.

Lewy, Hans. *Chaldean Oracles and Theurgy: Mysticism, Magic, and Platonism in the Later Roman Empire.* Nouvelle ed. Michel Tardieu. Paris: Etudes Augustiniennes, 1978.

Lienhard, J. T. "On 'Discernment of Spirits' in the Early Church." *Theological Studies* 41 (1980):505-529.

Lightstone, Jack N. *The Commerce of the Sacred: Mediation of the Divine among Jews in the Graeco-Roman Diaspora.* Brown Judaic Studies, no. 59. Chico, Calif.: Scholars Press, 1984.

Lubac, Henri de. *Histoire et Esprit: L'intelligence de l'Ecriture d'après Origène.* Théologie, no. 16. Paris: Aubier, 1950.

McCartney, Dan G. "Literal and Allegorical Interpretation in Origen's *Contra Celsum.*" *Westminster Theological Journal* 48 (1986):281-301.

Macleod, C. W. "ΑΝΑΛΥΣΙΣ: A Study in Ancient Mysticism." *Journal of Theological Studies* n.s. 21 (1970):43-55.

Marty, Francois. "Le discernement des esprits dans le Peri Archon d'Origène." *Revue d' ascetique et de mystique* 34 (1958):147-164, 253-274.

Meijering, E. P. "God, Cosmos, History: Christian and Neo-Platonic Views on Divine Revelation." *Vigiliae Christianae* 28 (1974):248-276.

Miller, Patricia Cox. " 'A Dubious Twilight': Reflections on Dreams in Patristic Literature." *Church History* 55 (1986):153-164.

Miura-Stange, Anna. *Celsus und Origenes: Das Gemeinsame ihrer Weltanschauung.* Zeitschrift für die neutestamentliche Wissenschaft, Beiheft 4. Gießen: Alfred Töpelmann, 1926.

Morrison, J.S. "The Classical World." In *Divination and Oracles*, pp. 87-114. Edited by Michael Loewe and Carmen Blacker. London: George Allen and Unwin, 1981.

Nardoni, Enrique. "Origen's Concept of Biblical Inspiration." *The Second Century* 4 (1984):9-23.

Nestle, Wilhelm. "Die Haupteinwände des antiken Denkens gegen das Christentum." *Archiv für Religionswissenchaft* 37 (1941/42):51-100.

Nilsson, Martin. *Greek Piety.* Oxford: Clarendon, 1948.

Pagels, Elaine H. "Christian Apologists and the 'Fall of the Angels': An Attack on Roman Imperial Power?" *Harvard Theological Review* 78 (1985):301-25.

_____. "Origen and the Prophets of Israel: A Critique of Christian Typology." *Journal of the Ancient Near Eastern Society of Columbia University* 5 (1973):335-344.

Pernveden, Lage. *The Concept of the Church in the Shepherd of Hermas.* Lund: Gleerup, 1966.

Pfeffer, Friedrich. *Studien zur Mantik in der Philosophie der Antike.* Beiträge zur klassischen Philologie, Heft 64. Meisenheim am Glan: Anton Hain, 1976.

Pichler, Karl. *Streit um das Christentum: Der Angriff des Kelsos und die Antwort des Origenes.* Regensburger Studien zur Theologie, Band 23. Frankfurt am Main: Peter Lang, 1980.

Pierre, Marie-Joseph. "L'âme dans l'anthropologie d'Origène." *Proche Orient Chrétien* 34 (1984):21-65.

Puech, Aimé. *Les apologistes Grecs du IIe siècle de notre ère.* Paris: Librairie Hachette, 1912.

Puiggali, Jacques. "La démonologie de Philostrate." *Revue des sciences philosophique et theologique* 67 (1983):117-130.

Rahner, Karl. "Le début d'une doctrine des cinq sens spirituels chez Origène." *Revue d'ascetique et de mystique* 13 (1932):113-145.

Reiling, Jannes. *Hermas and Christian Prophecy.* Supplements to Novum Testamentum, no. 37. Leiden: E. J. Brill, 1973.

_____. "Use of 'Pseudoprophetes' in the Septuagint, Philo, and Josephus." *Novum Testamentum* 13 (1971):147-156.

Remus, Harold. *Pagan-Christian Conflict over Miracle in the Second Century.* Philadelphia Patristic Monograph Series no. 10. Cambridge: Philadelphia Patristic Foundation, 1983.

_____. "Does Terminology Distinguish Early Christian from Pagan Miracles?" *Journal of Biblical Literature* 101 (1982):531-551.

Rohde, Erwin. *Psyche: The Cult of Souls and Belief in Immortality among the Greeks.* New York: Harcourt, Brace & Co., 1925.

Romaniuk, Kazimierz. "Le Platon d'Origène." *Aegyptus* 41 (1961):44-73.

Rougier, Louis. *Celse contre les Chrétiennes: La réaction païenne sous l'empire Romain.* Théoriques, vol. 1. Paris: Copernic, 1977.

Schröder, Heinrich Otto. "Celsus und Porphyrius als Christengegner." *Die Welt als Geschichte* 17 (1957):190-202.

Schwartz, Jacques. "Celsus redivivus." *Revue d'histoire et de philosophie religieuse* 53 (1973):399-405.

_____. "Du Testament de Lévi au Discours véritable de Celse." *Revue d'histoire et de philosophie religieuses* 40 (1960):126-145.

_____. "L'Epitre a Diognète." *Revue d'histoire et de philosophie religieuse* 48 (1968):46-53.

Segal, A.F. "Hellenistic Magic: Some Questions of Definition." In *Studies in Gnosticism and Hellenistic Religions, presented to Gilles Quispel*, pp. 349-375. Edited by R. van den Broek, and M. M. Vermaseren. Leiden: E.J. Brill, 1981.

Seitz, O.J.F. "Afterthoughts on the Term 'Dipsychos'." *New Testament Studies* 4 (1958):327-334.

_____. "Antecedents and Signification of the Term Δίψυχος." *Journal of Biblical Literature* 66 (1947):211-219.

_____. "Relationship of the Shepherd of Hermas to the Epistle of James." *Journal of Biblical Literature* 63 (1944):131-140.

Skarsaune, Oskar. *The Proof from Prophecy: A Study in Justin Martyr's Proof-Text Tradition. Text-Type, Provenance, Theological Profile*. Leiden: E.J. Brill, 1987.

Smith, Jonathan Z. "Towards Interpreting Demonic Powers in Hellenistic and Roman Antiquity." In *Aufstieg und Niedergang der romischen Welt*, II.16.1, pp. 425-439.

Smith, Morton. "On the History of the Divine Man." In *Paganisme, Judaisme, Christianisme: Mélanges offerts à Marcel Simon*, pp. 335-345. Paris: E. de Boccard, 1978.

Smith, Robert C., and Lounibos, John, eds. *Pagan and Christian Anxiety: A Response to E.R. Dodds*. Lanham: University Press of America, 1984.

Smith, Wesley D. "So-called Possession in Pre-Christian Greece." *Transactions and Proceedings of the American Philological Association* 96 (1965):403-426.

Sperduti, A. "The Divine Nature of Poetry in Antiquity." *Transactions of the American Philological Association* 81 (1950):209-240.

Stephanou, E. A. "The Charismata in the Early Church Fathers." *Greek Orthodox Theological Review* 21 (1976):125-146.

Stoike, Donald A. "De Genio Socratis (Moralia 575 A -- 598 F)." In *Plutarch's Theological Writing and Early Christianity*, pp. 236-285. Edited by Hans Dieter Betz. Leiden: E.J. Brill, 1975.

Tiede, David Lenz. *The Charismatic Figure as Miracle Worker*. Society of Biblical Literature Dissertation Series 1. Missoula, Montana: Society of Biblical Literature, 1972.

Trigg, Joseph W. "The Charismatic Intellectual: Origen's Understanding of Religious Leadership." *Church History* 50 (1981):5-19.

_____. *Origen: The Bible and Philosophy in the Third-Century Church*. Atlanta: John Knox Press, 1983.

_____. Review of *Celsus: On The True Doctrine*, by R. Joseph Hoffmann. *Church History* 57 (1988):353-354.

Ullmann, Walter. "Die Bedeutung der Gotteserkenntnis für die Gesamtkonzeption von Celsus' Logos alethes." *Studia Patristica* 14 (1975/76):180-188.

Unnik, W .C. van. "A Formula Describing Prophecy." *New Testament Studies* 9 (1962):86-94.

Vermander, Jean-Marie. "Celse, source et adversaire de Minucius Felix." *Revue des études Augustiniennes* 17 (1971):13-25.

_____. "La parution de l'ouvrage de Celse et la datation de quelques apologies." *Revue des études Augustiniennes* 18 (1972):27-42.

_____. "De quelques répliques à Celse dans le *Protreptique* de Clément d'Alexandria." *Revue des études Augustiniennes* 23 9(1977):3-17.

_____. "De quelques répliques à Celse dans l'*Apologeticum* de Tertullien." *Revue des études Augustiniennes* 16 (1970):205-225.

_____. "Théophile d'Antioche contre Celse: *A Autolycus* III." *Revue des études Augustiniennes* 17 (1971):203-225.

Vicaire, Paul. "Platon et la divination." *Revue des études Grecques* 83 (1970):333-350.

Völker, Walter. *Das Vollkommenheitsideal des Origenes*. Beiträge zur historischen Theologie, no. 7. Tübingen: J.C. B. Mohr, 1931.

Waszink, J. H. Review of *Logos und Nomos*, by Carl Andresen. *Vigiliae Christianae* 12 (1958):166-177.

_____. "La théorie du langage des dieux et des démons dans Calcidius." In *Epekstasis: Melanges patristiques offerts au Cardinal Jean Danielou*, pp. 237-244. Paris: Beauchesne, 1972.

Wey, Heinrich. *Die Funktionen der bösen Geister bei den griechishen Apologeten des zweiten Jahrhunderts nach Christus*. Winterthur: P.G. Keller, 1957.

Whittaker, John. "Plutarch, Platonism, and Christianity." In *Neoplatonism and Early Christian Thought: Essays in Honour of A.H. Armstrong*, pp. 50-63. Edited by H.J. Blumenthal and R.A. Markus. London: Variorum, 1981.

Wifstrand, Albert. "Die wahre Lehre des Kelsos." *Bulletin de la Société Royale des Lettres de Lund* (1941-42):391-431; *Humanistiska vetenskapssamfundet i. Lund. Arsberattelse.*

Wilken, Robert. *The Christians as the Romans Saw Them.* New Haven: Yale Univ. Press, 1984.

_____. "Religious Pluralism and Early Christian Theology." *Interpretation* 40 (1986):379-391.

Wilson, Robert R. *Prophecy and Society in Ancient Israel.* Philadelphia: Fortress, 1980.

Zöllig, August. *Die Inspirationslehre des Origenes.* Strassburger theologische Studien, fünfter Band. Freiburg: Herder, 1902.

DATE DUE

MAY 30 '91		
JUL 2 1994		
DEC 6 '98		
NOV 23 '98		

HIGHSMITH # 45220